I WILL BE YOUR GOD

I WILL BE YOUR GOD

A LAYMAN'S GUIDE TO OLD TESTAMENT STUDY

JOHN H. OTWELL

NASHVILLE   ABINGDON PRESS   NEW YORK

63495

PREFACE

The study of the Old Testament is rewarding and exciting. The New Testament takes on richer, fuller, and more profound meaning when we come to it with a knowledge of its background. But we also are not long in discovering that the Old Testament has worth in its own right. Its authors dealt with the ultimate questions of life in a direct, vivid, and warmly human way, stating beliefs which still challenge and enrich our lives.

I Will Be Your God, A Layman's Guide to Old Testament Study has been written for the inquiring layman who would like to make the Old Testament a part of his heritage. In every stage of its preparation it has been submitted to critics whose comments have proved to be most helpful. Four clergymen, Josh Wilson, Donald Anderson, Thomas Mann, and Robert Leland read carefully a preliminary draft; and Mrs. Robert Leland added her comments to those made by her husband. A later draft was read by Fred Stolp, a thoughtful student on the threshhold of study in the University of California. At every stage, my wife—to whom *I Will Be Your God* is dedicated—has carried major responsibilities. Without her it would never have been written.

7

Indebtedness to scholars is too vast to be acknowledged except in a few cases. All scholarship builds upon the work of others. A particular tribute, however, must be paid to the men who provided the translation of the Bible quoted throughout, the Revised Standard Version. The sources of other quoted materials are indicated in the footnotes.

Three convictions lie behind *I Will Be Your God:* that a knowledge of the Old Testament is necessary for vital Christian faith; that laymen when informed are capable of serious theological thought; and that the vitality of the church depends upon the presence of widespread, responsible lay theological thought.

These convictions were shared by the members of the 1963 Curriculum Committee of the Commission on Young Churchmen of the Christian Churches of Northern California-Nevada, the four clergymen named here in an earlier paragraph. The result was an ecumenical enterprise. An experimental edition of *I Will Be Your God* was written for this commission by a Methodist. After it had been tested, it was thoroughly revised and enlarged and is now being presented for the use of the general reader.

JOHN H. OTWELL

CONTENTS

INTRODUCTION

The layman who wishes to study the Bible as it has come to be known through modern scholarship faces the results of more than a century of brilliant, diligent, and detailed study. The sheer bulk of the materials available overwhelms everyone but the specialist, and sometimes even him! Therefore it is little wonder that many laymen decide either to be content with their memories of Sunday school lessons or to surrender quietly their budding interest. Even texts written for college students are still texts, and they presuppose the discipline of assignments and examinations to help master their multitude of details.

What is needed is a road map, so to speak: a presentation of the major outlines of a scholarly position in a form designed to explain how conclusions are reached, to describe the major historical and theological results found, and to encourage further study in those areas in which the reader finds himself taking particular interest. A road map gives us a view of the situation as a whole at the same time that it directs us to any area we wish to explore in detail for ourselves. A layman's introduction to the study of the Old Testament should serve the same functions.

I Will Be Your God is intended to fill this need. It opens with a description of the methods used in modern biblical scholarship and then gives briefly a "History of Traditions School" analysis of the structure, composition, and purpose of the Hexateuch (Genesis—Joshua), the Historical Books, the Great Prophets, Psalms, and the Wisdom Books (Proverbs, Job, and Ecclesiastes). The final chapter deals with the problem of the truth of the Bible.

In this kind of a study, it is as important to understand as to remember. The kind of material that can be learned by rote can always be looked up when needed. Since it changes constantly as new discoveries are made, it is better to know how it is discovered and why it is changed than it is to master the currently acceptable series of "facts." Endless confusion has been caused by the failure to remember that all scholarship is in a state of constant change. No set of results ever is eternal. Learn the rules governing scholarship, therefore, and thus learn how to understand and to judge what you read. In that which follows, as much care has been taken to explain why conclusions have been reached as to describe them. Analogy to more familiar areas of life has been used freely and without apology.

The history of biblical scholarship is a fascinating chapter in the intellectual history of Western man, but it has proved impossible to review it here. For the sake of the record, however, a word should be said about the History of Traditions School.

By 1900, over a century of increasingly detailed studies found a largely harmonious synthesis, in the description of the way the Old Testament had been written and its meaning, which is called the Graf-Wellhausen School—so-called because its founders were H. K. Graf and J. Wellhausen. The first five books of the Old Testament were believed to be a mosaic of four great sources (J, E, D, and P) dating from the time of David and Solomon for J (about 950 B.C.) to about 400 B.C. for P; and ranging from a primitive, naïve faith, only a little removed from paganism, to a lofty, ethical monotheism, one stage below Christianity. The rest of the books of the Old Testament were believed to be made up of original material expanded by later, and usually lesser, writers. Each book—and its "editors'" work—was fitted into the evolutionary scheme of Israelite faith just described. The great prophets were held to be the men whose religious genius was the means by which God had transformed the primitive faith of old Israel into the ethical monotheism out of which Jesus Christ emerged.

The Graf-Wellhausen School included many brilliant scholars, and its achievements will be respected and used for a long time to come. Several books illustrate its richness and variety. A description of its views on the authorship, date, purpose, and meaning of each book, or part of book, in the Old Testament was provided in Julius A. Bewer, *The Literature of the Old Testament*.[1] A historical description of Israel's religion as reconstructed by this school was provided in W. O. E. Oesterley and T. H. Robinson, *Hebrew Religion, Its Origin and Development*.[2] *A History of Israel*, by Robinson and Oesterley, is a splendid example of a political history of ancient Israel using the results of the Graf-Wellhausen School's researches.[3] Harry Emerson Fosdick, *A Guide to Understanding the Bible; the Development of Ideas Within the Old and New Testaments*,[4] is probably the product of the school most widely known in the United States. It presented the ethical and theological results in a form agreeable to the general intellectual climate of its day. For the English-speaking world, the climax of the Graf-Wellhausen School was undoubtedly reached in the detailed, learned scholarship poured into *The International Critical Commentary*. The most recent volume of this appeared in 1951,[5] and the series has never been completed.

This brief survey of the views and sample of the publications of the Graf-Wellhausen School is at least enough to give some idea of its inclusiveness and huge output. Increasingly, however, advanced studies were turning up material which could no longer be fitted into the school's position. In general, its spokesmen felt that our Bible began as a written literature even though its authors used oral and written traditions. More recent studies indicated the strong possibility that parts, at least, of our Bible took their present form as oral "literature." In general, spokesmen for the Graf-Wellhausen School felt that the authors of the Old Testament were as distinctively individual and rational as modern writers are. More recent studies failed to find evidence for such individualism and rationality but found instead evidence of intense cultic activity. In general, spokesmen for the Graf-Wellhausen School were convinced that the Old Testament displayed clearly the evolution of Israel's religion from primitive beginnings to advanced conclusions. Change clearly is present, but modern scholars are far less sure that the beginnings were as primitive, or the conclusions as advanced, as once thought.

Gradually, new information and new insights which could not be used in the Graf-Wellhausen position accumulated in such quantity that a new explanation of the makeup and meaning of the Old Testament became necessary. One of those proposed, and the one presented in the pages that follow, is called the History of Traditions School.

This school was founded largely by Albrecht Alt and two of his students, Gerhard von Rad and Martin Noth. Today, it is represented not only by these three and their students, but by many who have become converts through independent study.

Results of the application of the views of this school to the study of the Old Testament will be seen in the following chapters. Here a word should be said about the relationship between freedom of thought and the existence of schools of thought. This is a problem for us because of our devotion to the ideal of freedom of inquiry and our suspicion that partisanship limits such freedom.

The truth is that all inquiry is carried out within a framework of ideas. The nuclear physicist is guided by certain broad outlines of meaning as he sets up a problem, gathers data, and interprets it. He thinks in a world dominated at present by relativity and indeterminacy, to list two elements in his thought-world. That which marks off a helpful use of a school of thought from a destructive dependence upon it is the degree to which our relationship to the school is open. If our partisanship blinds us to information our viewpoint cannot use, the relationship is destructive. If, however, we use our "school" merely to keep our mental house in order—so to speak—while we struggle for more knowledge and more understanding, belonging to a school of thought becomes the alternative to being confused by details. Most of us have found that we are able to appreciate work done by those who belong to other schools than our own. Our own school of thought merely gives us the classroom in which we learn from all who would teach us. But we do need that classroom!

Introduction

The Revised Standard Version has been quoted throughout, and the Oxford Annotated Bible edition[6] is recommended because it includes introductions for each book of the Bible, explanatory footnotes for many obscure verses, phrases and terms, and also maps. The work was done carefully by responsible scholars. Older aids to Bible study have become outmoded by recent scholarship and confuse more than they help. Whenever the Lord, or God, is printed as LORD or GOD, the Hebrew text uses Yahweh, the Israelite proper name for God. Knowing that this intimate form of address is present often is important in our understanding of the meaning of a passage. The abbreviations for the titles of biblical books are those proposed by the translators of the Revised Standard Version.

Notes not only indicate the source of material, they also are used to suggest further study should you wish to pursue a specific question. Material judged to be common to all serious biblical scholarship usually has not been documented.

A final word about scholarly and theological controversy. Neither has been avoided here. We are men and not God. All our knowledge is imperfect, and there will be an end to controversy only when we "shall understand fully, even as [we] have been understood."

NOTES

1. (Rev. ed.; New York: Columbia University Press, 1933.) This kind of work is called an "introduction," and the two most inclusive and authoritative introductions produced by the Graf-Wellhausen School were: Robert H. Pfeiffer, *Introduction to the Old Testament* (New York: Harper & Brothers, 1941), and Otto Eissfeldt, *Einleitung in das Alte Testament* (Tübingen: J. C. B. Mohr [Paul Siebeck], 1934). In later editions, Professor Eissfeldt has modified his earlier work, as in the 3rd ed., published in English translation as *The Old Testament, an Introduction*, P. R. Ackroyd, tr. (New York: Harper & Row, 1965).
2. (New York: The Macmillan Company, 1930.) We turn again to Pfeiffer for one of the most detailed and comprehensive statements of

15

this. See his *Religion in the Old Testament: the History of a Spiritual Triumph* (New York: Harper & Brothers, 1961).

3. (2 vols.; Oxford: The Clarendon Press, 1932.)
4. (New York: Harper & Brothers, 1938.)
5. James A. Montgomery, *A Critical and Exegetical Commentary on the Books of Kings* (New York: Charles Scribner's Sons, 1951). Publication of the series began with S. R. Driver's volume on Deuteronomy issued in 1895.
6. (New York: Oxford University Press, 1962.)

THE LITERATURE OF THE OLD TESTAMENT

I

THE LITERATURE OF THE OLD TESTAMENT

1

When the ancient Israelite sage said, "Of making many books there is no end" (Eccles. 12:12), he might have added, of the revising and rewriting of books there also is no end. I once pictured an author as someone who sat in gentlemanly ease at a writing desk while literature flowed easily from his pen, but writing is hard work. It requires the careful formation of a structure of ideas, the careful phrasing of sentences, and the constant revising of both.

This is the way it is done when only one person is the author, but there are many times when more than one person has shared in writing a book. Some years ago, the distinguished American Old Testament scholar J. M. P. Smith wrote *The Prophets and Their Times*. Fifteen years later, the editors of the University of Chicago Press asked William A. Irwin, Professor Smith's successor, to revise it in the light of more recent scholarship. A comparison of the two editions will show quickly how much difference the work of a second author can make.

The first important example of this comes in the last paragraph of the first chapter. Since it is nearly three pages long in the second edition, we can quote only part of it here. The words added in the second edition are given in italics. Words which are present only in the first edition are enclosed in parentheses.

There is no sharp break between the early prophets and the great prophets of later times. The transition from early prophecy to later was a process of normal, natural growth. The prophets grew with the nation. As the nation was drawn more and more into the whirl of international politics, the outlook of the prophets widened (and)

17

their faith deepened; (but they retained the fundamental characteristics of prophecy to the very end.), *and the nature of their prophesying gradually underwent a transformation. Certain fundamental characteristics were retained to the end, but one has only to compare the mad fellows of Saul's day with the serious thoughtfulness and rational methods of men such as Habakkuk and Jeremiah to realize the immense distance that separates Israel's great prophecy from its rude beginnings.* . . . The prophets felt themselves to be in a very real sense partners with Yahweh in his great work, they expected to hear his voice of inspiration and instruction; and they heard it.[1]

If we compared the footnotes in the two editions, we would discover that Professor Irwin listed thirteen books and articles which had not appeared in print when Professor Smith was writing. These thirteen titles reflect a major change in scholarly activity. A study of the psychological state of the prophet had been begun by German thinkers several years earlier, and it could no longer be ignored when the second edition of *The Prophets and Their Times* was prepared. But if you were trying to understand Professor Smith's views on the nature of prophecy, and if you had available to you only the second edition of this book, you could be very wrong indeed in your conclusions if you did not know which words were those written by Professor Smith and which were those added by Professor Irwin.

There are also times when the authorship and even the purpose of a writing is hidden. On April 10, 1962, the *San Francisco Chronicle* carried a front-page article telling of the discovery of a bottle on the beach at Santa Cruz, California. It contained an appeal for help written on a page from a 1905 *Ayer's Almanac.* The author claimed to be shipwrecked on an island near San Francisco where he had lived for two months on grass and raw oysters. Did the message reveal an old tragedy, or was it a joke? Captain Ira Rubottom of the United States Coast and Geodetic Survey (which uses drifting bottles to trace ocean currents) thought it a joke, partly because he doubted whether any bottle would have drifted for so long unnoticed, and partly because he questioned whether a driftwood stopper would have lasted for so many years immersed in salt water.

It should be added that the Farallon Islands outside the Golden Gate (the only offshore islands near San Francisco) were occupied by a Coast Guard crew in 1903, and a castaway would probably have been found. Had the author of the note used "SOS" instead of "Help, Help, Help," doubts about it would have been even stronger, since SOS was first adopted as the international distress signal in 1912.

These two examples illustrate the basic problems that face us when we study the Old Testament. Those who have an "ear" for literary style discover that Isaiah 40–66 contains poetry which differs from the poetry in Isaiah 1–39, and that Isaiah 1–39 includes materials of various kinds. Since viewpoint is consistent within materials having the same style, but viewpoint changes as style changes, the reader who senses shifts in style begins eventually to suspect the presence of several authors in every book of the Old Testament, just as the two writers who prepared the two editions of *The Prophets and Their Times* can be detected by changes in style.

Furthermore, we need always to identify the kind of literature we are reading before we can understand it. We would have a quite different response to a note appealing for help if we thought it to be a joke than we would if we accepted it as authentic. For somewhat similar reasons we need to know, in reading the Old Testament, what we are reading. The Old Testament arose out of a life as varied and as vivid as our own, but it reflects that life in ways which change as the kind of literature being used changes. Is a passage the careful record of an event, or is it theology given us in the form of historical interpretation? Is a poem part of a liturgy describing changeless reality, or is it a prophetic condemnation arising out of a political crisis? What kind of literature is the passage, and what did its author try to tell us by his selection of this specific type of literature and not some other?

Christians have always believed that it is important to learn as much as possible about the Bible. The trouble has been that the ways of answering reliably questions about authorship, date, the kind of literature, and the original meaning have been discovered only fairly recently. Since the ways of answering these questions—called higher criticism—have been used to write these chapters, it is only fair to you to describe briefly how this science works. You do need to be warned, however, that biblical critics—those who apply the science of higher criticism to the Bible—do not know all the answers. There are many questions about which there is disagreement. There are others about which we simply do not have enough information with which to reach a conclusion. Nevertheless, the results thus far are exciting and useful. But remember, biblical critics do not have all the answers.

There are several individual tasks that a biblical critic performs. First, he tries to determine whether or not the letters and words in the biblical text are correct. This is called textual criticism. Next, he tries to answer the questions we asked earlier here: who was the author, to whom did he speak (or write), why did he speak (or write), when, what kind of literature did he use, precisely what did he say? This is called higher criticism. The tasks of those engaged in higher criticism, in their turn, are grouped into a series of methods which have various names. We will call them literary criticism (a shortened form of grammatico-literary criticism), historical criticism, patternism (sometimes called studies in comparative religions), and form criticism. "Criticism" here means careful, methodical study. It does not imply that one is being negative.

We will try to explain and to illustrate each of these methods in turn.

2

A. *The first to be described is literary criticism.*[2] The initial task facing the literary critic is to master the language in which a work is written so well that he can give a reliable report of what was being said. This demands that the scholar master the language historically. He must know all the rules of grammar through all their changes over several centuries of use; and he must know also how words changed their meanings across the years. In the King James Version, Psalm 119:147 does not seem to make much sense: "I prevented the dawning of the morning, and cried; I hoped in thy word." The same verse in the Revised Standard Version reads:

> I rise before dawn and cry for help;
> I hope in thy words.

Is one of these correct and the other wrong? Or, has the English language itself changed?

If I had a historical knowledge of English, I would know that "to prevent" in 1611, when the King James Version was translated, meant "to act before the time something else happened." Actually, therefore, both translations are saying the same thing in the vocabularies in use when each was translated. I could misunderstand a passage in the Hebrew Bible in the same way unless I had a historical knowledge of Hebrew. Basically, a historical knowledge of a language is knowing it in terms of its origins, its kinship to other similar languages, and its changes across the centuries.

The second task facing the literary critic is to study the style of writing in a work in order to discover how many authors it had, to compare the styles found in this book with the styles found in other books, and to group together passages from one or more books which have the same style. When he begins such a study, he often is helped in dividing a writing into its parts by abrupt changes in viewpoint or even in subject matter.

In this way the literary critic learns that one person wrote certain parts of a book or group of books. Style includes words a person uses over and over again (often the repeated choice of one word where any one of several might have served), the order of words, the grammatical constructions, and the phrases which appear repeatedly. One person might say "Oh no!" when he was dismayed, another when he was amused. This would be a stylistic trait. Literary criticism has been tested repeatedly in the study of modern literature and has been found to work.

You can try it for yourself. Read aloud the following passages a few times, listening to the sound of the words as you read. Or you can listen as a friend reads.

10) "I sent among you a pestilence after the manner of Egypt;
    I slew your young men with the sword;
    I carried away your horses;
       and I made the stench of your camp go up into your nostrils;
    yet you did not return to me,"
               says the LORD.

11) "I overthrew some of you,
    as when God overthrew Sodom and Gomorrah,
    and you were as a brand plucked out of the burning;
    yet you did not return to me,"
               says the LORD.

12) "Therefore thus I will do to you, O Israel;
    because I will do this to you,
    prepare to meet your God, O Israel!"

13) For lo, he who forms the mountains, and creates the wind,
    and declares to man what is his thought;
  who makes the morning darkness,
    and treads on the heights of the earth—
the LORD, the God of hosts, is his name!
               (Amos 4:10-13.)

Do you understand now why we say, solely on the basis of style, that Amos 4:13 is not the work of the same person who spoke the words preserved in Amos 4:10-12?

Now compare Amos 4:13, quoted above, with Amos 5:8-9, and 9:5-6.

5:8) He who made the Pleiades and Orion,
     and turns deep darkness into the morning,
     and darkens the day into night,
  who calls forth the waters of the sea,
     and pours them out upon the surface of the earth,
  the LORD is his name,
  9) who makes destruction flash forth against the strong,
     so that destruction comes upon the fortress.

9:5) The Lord, GOD of hosts
  he who touches the earth and it melts,
     and all who dwell in it mourn,
  and all of it rises like the Nile,
     and sinks again, like the Nile of Egypt;
  6) who builds his upper chambers in the heavens,
     and founds his vault upon the earth;
  who calls for the waters of the sea,
     and pours them out upon the surface of the earth—
  the LORD is his name.

Would you be willing to agree that all these verses were written by the same man? Would you even go so far as to say that Amos 4:13, 5:8-9, and 9:5-6 belong together, that they are parts of the same hymn? [3]

There is one more step. Read now Isaiah 40:21-23:

21) Have you not known? Have you not heard?
  Has it not been told you from the beginning?
  Have you not understood from the foundation of the earth?
22) It is he who sits above the circle of the earth,
     and its inhabitants are like grasshoppers;
  who stretches out the heavens like a curtain,
     and spreads them like a tent to dwell in;
23) who brings princes to nought,
     and makes the rulers of the earth as nothing.

If you agreed that Amos 4:10-12 was not by the same author who produced Amos 4:13, and if you also agreed that Amos 4:13;

23

5:8-9; and 9:5-6 have the same author; are you willing to assert now that the style in these five verses is closer to the style of Isaiah 40:21-23 than it is to the style of Amos 4:10-12? If we are in agreement, you have been using literary criticism!

B. *A second method of higher criticism is called historical criticism.*[4] This unfolds in three stages.

First, the reports of events preserved in the Old Testament are tested for their accuracy. Second, reports judged to be reliable are used to reconstruct as much of Israel's history as possible. And, finally, the reconstruction of Israel's history is used to date and to help interpret passages not believed themselves to be reports of events. Reports about Israel coming from outside the Old Testament but from the same age are included in the first two of these three steps.

Some of the rules used to determine the reliability of a report of an event are as follows. A reliable report is not written before the event happened. Details which did not exist when the event is said to have happened imply that the report was written at the time of the latest of the details. Trustworthy reports of the same event will agree in many ways, and their disagreements can be explained. Internal contradictions indicate either an unreliable narrative, or a narrative made by blending two or more, once independent and conflicting, stories. All materials reflecting a strong, consistent bias must have the bias discounted. The presence of fantastic, fanciful elements—features which contradict our knowledge of the way in which the universe operates—makes a narrative questionable.

Not everything which comes to us out of the past is an attempt to describe that past, just as not everything written today describes conditions today. We write novels and plays about the Civil War today; scientific works describe matter as it is, regardless of whether it is 1965 or 2093; and we write a good deal about what we think facts mean. So it is in the Old Testament. Parts

24

of it were never intended to describe the facts of Israelite history. Other parts are reactions to those facts. Still other passages are hymns, codes of law, and fiction. We need to know how to recognize the kinds of literature which are primarily reports of facts in order to distinguish them from all the rest. Then we test alleged reports of facts in the way just described in order to test their reliability. This is the first stage of historical criticism.

The second stage is to prepare the factual narrative. This is much like putting together a jigsaw puzzle with many of the pieces missing. The historical critic is always helped greatly by the fact that the events he seeks to report happened in time. This means that event A either happened before event B, at the same time as B, or later than B. The relationship in time gives the backbone of the reconstruction—if a jigsaw puzzle could be said to have a backbone. But that alone is not enough.

A boy telling how he got his black eye may get everything he tells in the right order and still omit a few important steps. He was just walking down the street when he saw Murgatroyd, and Murgatroyd came up and smote him a fearful blow—to use a bit of biblical language. One bit of information is missing—that he greeted Murgatroyd in just a certain way—which changes the report a good deal. Nothing was said which was untrue. It was merely a bit limited. But a wise mother develops an ear for the unspoken parts of a story before she allows her maternal instincts to rise to fighting pitch.

Old Testament historians constantly must deal with narratives lacking bits and pieces—and sometimes chunks and blocks. This need not be the result of slanted reporting. Accident in passing the report from generation to generation can be the cause of the loss of important information. Whatever the cause for it, the biblical historian usually has only a part of the story. He has reports of some of the events, he can date some of the events in relationship to other events, and he can see some of the kinships that exist between events. What he does not know must be filled in before he can write a reasonably complete account. He often must do what the wise mother does. He deduces from a known event its probable result; from that he moves to the next known event which could be the result of the conjectured event. Whatever is done, the rule is always the same: move from what is known into the unknown, governed by possibility.

The third stage of historical criticism is the attempt to date passages which do not refer to events. Two methods dominate here. First, when a unique style and viewpoint is shared by several passages, one of which can be dated, the date given the dated passage is given all like material. Isaiah 44:24–45:8 refers to the invasion of Babylonia by Cyrus the Great in 536 B.C. Since Isaiah 40–55 has the same style and viewpoint, all sixteen chapters are given the date assigned Isaiah 44:24–45:8. Second, when only hints to events are present, a passage is given the date which seems most suitable in light of known history. Jeremiah 2:2-3 does not refer to an event, but it implies that the prophet believed that Israel again pleased God as it had during the Exodus. In Jeremiah's lifetime, such an attitude would seem most appropriate early in the Deuteronomic Reformation, before the prophet became disillusioned.

Historical criticism can seem to produce more than it has. It is intended to determine whether or not a report of an event or belief is a correct report, not whether it is a correct belief. The historical critic might conclude that Isaiah 1:4-9 is both an accurate description of the Assyrian devastation of Judah in 701 B.C. and an accurate report of Isaiah's interpretation of the significance of the invasion. It also is very important to decide whether or not Isaiah was right in holding that Yahweh was acting in the Assyrian invasion described in Isaiah 1:4-9. The historical critic cannot answer this question in his role as a historical critic.

In Genesis 14:14, we are told that Abram pursued an enemy as far as Dan. Dan was an Israelite tribe which lived originally along the seacoast northwest of Jerusalem. It moved north after another

Israelite tribe pushed it out of its territory. The tribe of Dan then captured Laish, renaming it Dan. The story is told in Judges 17:1–18:31. We are most interested here in Judges 18:27-29:

(27) And taking what Micah had made, and the priest who belonged to him, the Danites came to Laish, to a people quiet and unsuspecting, and smote them with the edge of the sword, and burned the city with fire. (28) And there was no deliverer because it was far from Sidon, and they had no dealings with any one. It was in the valley which belongs to Beth-rehob. And they rebuilt the city, and dwelt in it. (29) And they named the city Dan, after the name of Dan their ancestor, who was born to Israel; but the name of the city was Laish at the first.

Since Genesis 14:14 asserts that Abram pursued an enemy as far north as the city of Dan, the statement could not have been written before the tribe of Dan existed, before it had entered Palestine, before it had moved north, or before it had captured and renamed Laish. Genesis 14:14 is not a prediction. It is simply a casual reference to a place name which the author and his readers both knew. We cannot date this passage except to say that it was written after the capture and renaming of Laish. But this would have been centuries after the time of Abram, since the tribe of Dan is said to have been distant descendants of Abram.

Isaiah 40:1–55:13 has already been mentioned. These fifteen chapters have the same style and probably are the work of one man. We do not know his name, although it is plain that he was the greatest thinker, one of the finest poets, and one of the greatest of the prophets of the Old Testament. Literary criticism makes us decide that these chapters are not the work of a prophet named Isaiah ben Amoz, who gave the sermons reported in some of the earlier chapters of the book of Isaiah. Historical criticism also makes us conclude that the two parts of the book did not come from the same person.

Isaiah 7:1-9 refers to a war that took place in 734 B.C. The names of the three kings involved are given in verses 3 and 4:

(3) And the LORD said to Isaiah, "Go forth to meet Ahaz, you and Shearjashub your son, at the end of the conduit of the upper pool on the highway to the Fuller's Field, (4) and say to him, 'Take heed, be quiet, do not fear, and do not let your heart be faint because of these two smoldering stumps of firebrands, at the fierce anger of Rezin and Syria and the son of Remaliah.'"

Ahaz was the king of Judah, Rezin was the king of Syria, and the king of Israel—named Pekah according to 2 Kings 16:1—was "the son of Remaliah." The brief war these kings fought took place in 734 B.C. Isaiah 44:28–45:1 also names a king, but he is Cyrus the Great.

> 44:28) "who says of Cyrus, 'He is my shepherd,
> and he shall fulfill all my purpose';
> saying of Jerusalem, 'She shall be built,'
> and of the temple, 'Your foundation shall be
> laid.'"
> 45:1) Thus says the LORD to his anointed, to Cyrus,
> whose right hand I have grasped,
> to subdue nations before him
> and ungird the loins of kings,
> to open doors before him
> that gates may not be closed.

Cyrus overthrew the second Babylonian Empire in 539 B.C. and founded the Persian Empire. He became powerful very swiftly (between 549 and 539). The biblical passage is not a prediction of a distant future. The Lord has already grasped Cyrus by the hand, according to the prophet. This must be taken as a reference to a king living at the same time as the prophet and his readers. Therefore we date these references fairly close to 539 B.C.

The results of historical criticism here coincide with the results of literary criticism. The prophet who gave his name to the book of Isaiah was preaching in 701 B.C., but Isaiah 40:1–55:13 comes from another prophet writing over 150 years later, about 540.

One more example. The peace terms imposed by the victorious Assyrians on King Hezekiah in 701 B.C. are given in 2 Kings 18:14-16.

(14) And Hezekiah king of Judah sent to the king of Assyria at Lachish, saying, "I have done wrong; withdraw from me; whatever you impose on me I will bear." And the king of Assyria required of Hezekiah king of Judah three hundred talents of silver and thirty talents of gold. (15) And Hezekiah gave him all the silver that was found in the house of the LORD, and in the treasuries of the king's house. (16) At that time Hezekiah stripped the gold from the doors of the temple of the LORD, and from the doorposts which Hezekiah king of Judah had overlaid and gave it to the king of Assyria.

We also have the victor's account of these same terms, and a comparison is interesting. This is the Assyrian report.

Hezekiah . . . did send me, later, to Nineveh, my lordly city, together with 30 talents of gold, 800 talents of silver, precious stones, antimony, large cuts of red stone, couches (inlaid) with ivory, *nímedu*-chairs (inlaid) with ivory, elephant-hides, ebony-wood, box-wood, and all kinds of valuable treasures, his own daughters, concubines, male and female musicians.[5]

A talent was a measure of weight, about 75.5 pounds in Hezekiah's day. Since it is fairly probable that gold then was worth a good deal more than it is today, you can estimate for yourself that Hezekiah paid a large tribute, whether you take the smaller or the larger description of it. The two accounts do not necessarily contradict each other. The biblical statement reports the tribute Hezekiah paid immediately, sending it to Lachish where the Assyrian was encamped. The Assyrian inscription adds to the tally of tribute that which was sent later to the Assyrian capital city.

C. *Patternism is sometimes called criticism by comparative religions.*[6] Most cultures have two traits: they are international, and they form a pattern. Patternism stresses both the international extent of the culture and the presence of pattern.

A culture is all that man has created: language, customs, morals, tools, art, government, recreations, and the like. In theory, one people alone might create a culture. In fact, all great cultures have been the work of many peoples over many centuries. The United States and Canada, for example, share in the culture of Western Europe. Modern Western European culture is the end product of centuries of growth in which many peoples contributed, some of whom did not even live in Western Europe—such as the ancient Israelites and modern Americans.

It was thought for centuries that the Old Testament reported a unique culture. This belief is now known to have been wrong. Linguists and archaeologists have proved that Israelite culture was a part of what is called Semitic culture. Biblical Hebrew is a Semitic dialect, closely related to Ugaritic, Akkadian, Aramaic, and Arabic. Much Old Testament law parallels Babylonian law. The pottery and tools found by archaeologists in ancient Israelite cities resemble earlier Canaanite pottery and tools. Many of the ideas stated in the Old Testament are found also in non-Israelite, ancient Semitic writings. The Israelites shared in a widely spread culture.

Cultures also reflect basic patterns. They have coherence. We use mechanical methods of travel today in Western European culture, and we value democracy at least in theory. Both of these are true for all the nations of the Western European cultural area. As a result, we try to make the same tools of travel available to everyone. The President of the United States uses precisely the same kinds of machines to travel as you do. Finding the basic traits of a culture and grouping them together in their patterns is widely practiced today.

The writers of the Old Testament assumed that their readers knew all about their culture. Their original readers did! When I read in a newspaper that the President sent a message to Congress, I do not need to be told who the President is, what his duties and the work of the Congress are, or why he would send Congress a message. Both the newspaper reporter and I know all these things because both of us share in the same culture. But I do not share the culture of the ancient Israelite. How do I go about understanding what the author of 2 Samuel 18:3 meant when he said:

But the men [of Israel] said [to David], "You shall not go out. For if we flee, they will not care about us. If half of us die, they will not care about us. But you are worth ten thousand of us; therefore it is better that you send us help from the city."

Criticism by patternism tries to correct my ignorance.

If enough is written, enough will be said by accident to make possible a reconstruction of at least a part of a culture. One newspaper reporter might call the President "the Chief Executive." Another reporter might refer to Congress as "the Legislature." When I read enough, I begin to pick up hints here and there. The President administers; the Congress passes laws. It is obvious that the two would have to work together. As soon as I begin to draw such conclusions as this, I am starting to reconstruct the pattern out of the hints. But remember that cultures are international. The hints being used can come from the remains left by all the peoples sharing the same culture.

If I read many ancient Semitic references to kings, I would soon discover that the king was held to be either divine or to be a special representative of the gods. He was thought to have special tasks. One of the most important of these was to bring the strength of the gods to the people, a strength concentrated in life itself. If the king failed to do this, the nation lost its divinely given strength. When the people told David that he was equal to ten thousand of them, they believed precisely what they said. If the divine power which they felt came through him were cut off by his being killed, not even the strength of ten thousand men could make up the loss.

This method of study is difficult to use. Specialists in patternism sometimes forget that a people not only shares in an international culture, it also uses parts of that culture in ways unique to it alone.

What is unique to the United States, in the political institutions we share with Western European nations, is as important as what is shared with those nations. What was unique to ancient Israel is the reason we study the Bible, rather than the sacred writings of the ancient Babylonians. When this is forgotten, the method becomes destructive. It also is very easy to misunderstand a culture other than one's own. In spite of these weaknesses, patternism is important. It serves as the tool by which we come to understand much of what we read in the Old Testament, as well as the means by which we isolate that which is unique to the Old Testament.

D. *The last method of higher criticism to be discussed here is form criticism.*[7] This is the most difficult of the methods to describe and to use. We have learned, partly through patternism, that the ancient Israelites had what is called an oral culture. They knew and used writing, but they memorized far more than we do. This is still true of many of the peoples that live in the lands of the Bible. Because they used their memories more than we do, they trained them better than we do. They also used certain fixed ways of expressing themselves which we call "forms." Do you know the difference between a joke and a limerick? Both of these are forms. A cheer used during a sporting event is a form, and so is the proper wording for a lease. A gospel hymn differs from a Christmas carol because each is a distinctive form. We have many different forms, proper ways of saying certain things under certain circumstances. We could write a lease in the form of a Christmas carol, but it would be easier and clearer to use the lease form.

The Old Testament—and also the New Testament—is filled with such forms. The task is to learn what they are, to identify the form used in a specific passage, and to discover the situation in which that particular form was normally used. This gets involved, as you can imagine. There is no one to tell us what these forms were, since the Jews themselves forgot centuries ago. It gets to be a little like hunting a black cat in the dark.

You will not need to know too much about form criticism—how to apply it, for example—but you will want to know that we can sometimes say that one description of an event is older than another because the form used in the first is more appropriate to an oral record, or more appropriate to the life situation being described; that we sometimes can say that a specific passage was used in a specific kind of situation because we can identify the form and know when that form was used. Even though this is all that you need to know for the following chapters, you may wish to look at a few examples. You have to remember, of course, that the Old Testament was written originally in Hebrew—with a few chapters and verses in Aramaic. Being able to study it in its original language sometimes makes a lot of difference.

The most important form in the study of the Psalms is the hymn. This usually has three parts: the summons to praise God, a description of why God is to be praised, and a return to the summons to praise God. A hymn could contain only the first part (as in Ps. 150), but it also could drop the first part and begin immediately with the description of why God is being praised (Ps. 114). Most hymns, however, have all three parts.

The summons to praise with which a hymn usually opened and closed could be a simple command, such as Psalm 113:1:

> Praise the LORD!
> Praise, O servants of the LORD,
> praise the name of the LORD!

The introduction also could include a fuller identification of the group asked to praise and a description of how it should praise God, as in Psalm 149:1-3:

> 1) Praise the Lord!
>   Sing to the LORD a new song,
>   his praise in the assembly of the
>   faithful!
> 2) Let Israel be glad in his Maker,

let the sons of Zion rejoice in
their King!
3) Let them praise his name with dancing,
making melody to him with timbrel
and lyre!

A few psalms include other works of God, such as the heavenly
bodies, in the congregation asked to praise him (Ps. 148:3-4).

When the congregation described its reasons for praising God,
three variations on one theme usually appear. The theme is a
review of the mighty acts of God by which he revealed his royal
power and will. These acts, however, were seen often in nature
(as in Pss. 29:3-9 and 33:6-7), in the events of Israel's history
(Pss. 47:3-4 and 114:1-6), or in a combination of the two (as in
Pss. 135:5-12 and 136:4-25).

Psalm 117 is the shortest of all of the psalms, yet it is a complete
hymn.

1) Praise the Lord, all nations!
Extol him, all peoples!
2) For great is his steadfast love toward us;
and the faithfulness of the Lord
endures for ever.
Praise the Lord!

Exodus 15:1-18 and 1 Samuel 2:1-10 are examples of hymns
now found outside the book of Psalms. The Second Isaiah, the
unknown prophet who wrote Isaiah 40–55, scattered little hymns
throughout his oracles, perhaps because he could not suppress his
joy. Isaiah 49:13 is one example:

Sing for joy, O heavens, and exult, O earth;
break forth, O mountains, into singing!
For the Lord has comforted his people,
and will have compassion on his afflicted.

In this hymn, heavens and earth are urged to praise God not only
for what he has done, but also for what he is about to do.

Another form which you can spot for yourself is the aphorism. This is a short saying in which the second half either repeats or reverses the first half. This is a form adopted by the sages, learned men who served as secretaries and advisers for kings and princes. The sages were professional men, and they established schools to train students in reading, writing, law, administration, and ethics. They taught many of these subjects by means of lists of aphorisms. The book of Proverbs in the Old Testament—as we will see later—is a collection of several such lists, and some of the aphorisms preserved there are shrewd. Consider these:

> Faithful are the wounds of a friend;
> profuse are the kisses of an enemy.
> (Prov. 27:6.)

> What is desired in a man is loyalty,
> and the poor man is better than a liar.
> (19:22.)

Humor appears sometimes also, as in the following:

> "It is bad, it is bad," says the buyer;
> but when he goes away, then he boasts.
> (20:14.)

> A stone is heavy, and sand is weighty,
> but a fool's provocation is heavier than both.
> (27:3.)

> He who blesses his neighbor with a loud voice,
> rising early in the morning,
> will be counted as cursing.
> (27:14.)

The aphorism is so closely linked with the sages that we assume that a sage was the author each time we meet one. Since the sages helped edit the prophetic books, they left some traces there of their activity. Hosea 14:9 is an example of this.

E. *One of the results of the use of historical criticism* has been the discovery that it cannot be applied as often in the study of the Old Testament as scholars had hoped. Part of the work of the historical critic is to decide whether or not a passage of scripture contains reliable information about the past. There are certain kinds of literature called legend, which do not lend themselves to study by the tools used by the historian. Such writings may or may not report the events of the past accurately. The historian has no way of determining this from the legends themselves. His conclusion has to be "no verdict."

Much of the Old Testament falls into categories the historians cannot use. This is true of the stories in the Pentateuch—the first five books of the Old Testament—Psalms, Proverbs, Job, and some parts of the historical books—Joshua, Judges, Samuel, Kings, Chronicles, Ezra, and Nehemiah—as well as such books as Ruth and Jonah. When biblical scholars first began to suspect this, there was a great deal of dismay.

Where they were able to apply their methods, historical critics made great contributions to our understanding of the Old Testament. The discovery that these methods often could not be used seemed to mean that there were many periods of biblical history which would always remain closed to us, and many passages in the Old Testament which could not be studied by means of higher criticism. A little thought, however, made the nature of the problem clear. Historical criticism had not been "disproved"; the limits of its usefulness had been learned. Some of the Old Testament could not be studied fruitfully with this tool. In other parts, there was so little information that the results of the use of historical criticism was unsure. What was needed was new, independent material to study, material which the historian could examine and to which he could apply his methods.

Archaeology fills this need. Archaeology is the recovery and the interpretation of the physical remains of ancient cultures. For the student of the Bible, this means recovering and interpreting buried remains of the cultures of the lands of the Bible which were contemporary to biblical history.

The results have been fantastic.[8] So much has been recovered that we know more today about the time of the Israelite monarchy than has any previous generation of Christians. Throughout much of the period covered by the books of Kings and Chronicles, the records of the Assyrian kings invading Palestine—records carved into stone during the reigns of the kings named—have been found, translated, and published. [9] This is the kind of material the rules of scientific historical analysis were designed to handle. The Old Testament historian who studies the Assyrian records critically has a second source of information to use alongside the historical materials in the Old Testament in his reconstruction of the history of the Israelite monarchy. The results of the critical examination of the Assyrian records help the biblical historian to judge the reliability and to define the nature of the Old Testament historical books. This is merely one example of the many that could be reported.

Nevertheless, it is possible to ask the archaeologist to do more than his science permits, just as historical critics are often asked "to prove" more than they can. To guard ourselves against asking for the impossible, we need to remember that the finds made by the archaeologists are raw materials which then must be studied by the historical critic before they can be used to reconstruct our knowledge of the past.

Historical criticism is a tool to help us to correct distortions in our records of the past. Archaeology recovers new records of great value, but merely because a record has only recently been rediscovered does not mean that it lacks the flaws found in long familiar records from the past. We haven't started making mistakes recently only, propaganda is not a a new invention, and familiar classics of ancient literature are not less reliable because they are familiar! All reports of past events need to be studied with the same care and respect, whether we have known about them for centuries or have just recently discovered them.

You now have had some hints of the way biblical scholars work. Before we finish with this first chapter, however, you need a brief summary of their findings. We must speak here in very general terms, going into greater detail later.

First, biblical criticism has discovered that every book in the Old Testament is the work of many authors. This is true even of the small books like Ruth or Jonah, although it isn't as much a problem there as in larger books. For the larger books, it is very important always to remember that these works were written by several persons. In some cases, the work of a single author extends through parts of several books.

This statement causes many people to have misgivings because they feel that it destroys the Bible. It does destroy our interpretation of the meaning of the arrangement of the Bible. Because we are familiar with books written by individuals, we assume that authorship by an individual has always been one of the parts of the definition of a book. We also have books which are collections of essays on a single theme written by different authors, and this is an alternative definition of a book. It is a body of writing which either has one author or one theme—or both a single author and a single theme. When, therefore, we find that the books of the Old Testament contain different themes, we conclude reasonably enough that they can be called books because they have one author.

But there is still another possibility. A book might be a convenient block of material, having several authors and discussing several kinds of subjects but being of a standard length. Have you ever noticed how many books of the Old Testament are of the same length? This becomes even stranger when you learn that the twelve Minor Prophets are all in one book in the Hebrew Bible, where they are called the Book of the Twelve. If you count the pages needed to print the four prophetic books of the Old Testament, you get this result. [10]

The Literature of the Old Testament

Prophetic Book	Length	
	Hebrew Bible	English Bible
Isaiah	93	74
Jeremiah	107	82
Ezekiel	84	115
The Book of the Twelve	82	115

Does this not look as if there had been a deliberate attempt to make the four great collections of prophetic sayings approximately the same length? Such a conclusion is strengthened when we remember that a handwritten manuscript could easily vary as much in length from one copying to the next as the differences shown above. Printing with movable type, of course, was not introduced until about A.D. 1440. It seems probable that the editors of the Old Testament intended each collection of prophetic sayings to be just long enough to fill one easily handled scroll. If this conclusion is correct, we have to say that the present division of the Old Testament into "books" was determined more by convenience in handling than by authorship. None of this need disturb us. If we want to know who wrote what, we use literary criticism.

Our second general conclusion about the Old Testament is that most of the collections of material in it cluster around a core of very old cultic traditions or the work of a giant who founded either a movement or a school. We will see shortly that old cultic traditions form the core of the Pentateuch. Isaiah, as an example of a leader founding a school, was the master of a band of disciples mentioned in Isaiah 8:16. The founder was greater than any of his followers, except the author of chapters 40–55. This does not mean that we reject the words of the disciples and seek only those of the master; rather we try to distinguish between the two, since they spoke out of different situations and to different problems.

The third general conclusion is that the whole of the Old

Testament deals with one question: how God has dealt with man in man's daily life. The Old Testament is not a book of scientific knowledge. We look to modern scientists for this kind of information. The Old Testament is not primarily a book of ancient history, although it comes out of the past and thus contains a lot of information we must use in writing ancient history. The Old Testament is not chiefly a book of beautiful literature, although it contains some superbly beautiful writing. The Old Testament is not even a handbook of ethics, even though it contains the Ten Commandments, many other wise laws, and many profound ethical insights. The Old Testament was intended to be the report of the struggle of a whole people to understand how God was dealing with it. It is talking about a life as real as the one you live. It reports failures along with insights. The Old Testament is one of the most honest, most complete accounts of the relationship between God and man that we have.

This means that it should be read like a newspaper, or studied like a textbook. We are reading about real living, not make-believe. The births and deaths, battles, revolutions, and taxes are all real. We will never understand it if we sit down in a special "religious" position, force our minds to start thinking in a special "religious" way, and read aloud in a special "religious" tone of voice. Read first of all to enjoy and to understand. Then do yourself the honor of thinking as hard as you can about what you have read. Let God worry about speaking to you through your struggle to understand. He can fend for himself!

NOTES

1. J. M. P. Smith, *The Prophets and Their Times* (Chicago: University of Chicago Press, 1925; rev. ed., edited by William A. Irwin, 1941), p. 11 of the 1st ed. and pp. 12-14 of the 2nd ed.
2. One of the most widely respected examples of the use of literary criticism is S. R. Driver, *An Introduction to the Literature of the Old Testament* (New York: Charles Scribner's Sons, [1891], 1913). Also available in paperback (Meridian). See pp. 131-35 for an example of the results of

the use of literary criticism. Consult J. Estlin Carpenter, *The Composition of the Hexateuch: An Introduction with Select Lists of Words and Phrases* (London: Longmans, Green & Co., 1902), pp. 101-12 for an explanation of the method, and pp. 381-425 for lists of words and phrases associated with different sources found in the Hexateuch. C. A. Simpson, *The Early Traditions of Israel: A Critical Analysis of the Pre-Deuteronomic Narrative of the Hexateuch* (New York: The Macmillan Company, 1948), is a more recent example of the intensive use of literary criticism.

3. To the best of my knowledge, first proposed on the basis of a study of poetic meter by Bernhard Duhm. See Duhm's *The Twelve Prophets: A Version in the Various Poetical Measures of Original Writings,* Archibald Duff, tr. (London: A & C. Black, 1912), pp. 66 ff., originally published as *Die zwölf Propheten: in den Versmassen der Urschrift* (Tübingen: J. C. B. Mohr [Paul Siebeck], 1910).

4. Histories of the Old Testament period are based upon the results of the use of historical criticism. Three widely used histories are available in English: T. H. Robinson and W. O. E. Oesterley, *A History of Israel* (2 vols.; Oxford: The Clarendon Press, 1932), a work using literary and historical criticism; Martin Noth, *The History of Israel,* S. Godman tr. (New York: Harper & Row [1958] 1960), a work using form criticism in addition to literary and historical criticism; and John Bright, *A History of Israel* (Philadelphia: The Westminster Press, 1959), a work which is consistently more cautious than either of the others listed here but making more use of archaeological data. Sidney Smith, *Isaiah, Chapters XL–LV: Literary Criticism and History* (London: Oxford University Press [H. Milford, published for the British Academy], 1944), is an example of a detailed application of the method to a part of the Old Testament.

5. Leo Oppenheim, tr., "Babylonian and Assyrian Historical Texts," in James B. Pritchard, ed., *Ancient Near Eastern Texts Relating to the Old Testament* (2nd ed., rev.; copyright Princeton University Press, 1955), p. 288; found also in Pritchard, ed., *The Ancient Near East, an Anthology of Texts and Pictures* (Princeton: Princeton University Press, 1958), pp. 200-201. Material in square brackets is lacking in the inscription and has been supplied by the translator by conjecture; material in parentheses is an insertion made by the translator for clarity; material in italics is a conjectural translation.

6. Patternism is illustrated by Theodore H. Gaster, *Thespis: Ritual, Myth and Drama in the Ancient Near East* (Garden City: Doubleday Anchor Books, 1961); and S. H. Hooke, ed., *Myth and Ritual: Essays on the Myth and Ritual of the Hebrews in Relation to the Culture Pattern of the Ancient East* (London: Oxford University Press, 1933). The Introduction by Hooke contains a statement of the method, and the essays by various scholars which follow illustrate the use of it. So also do the

essays in two other symposia edited by Hooke: *The Labyrinth: Further Studies in the Relation Between Myth and Ritual in the Ancient World* (New York: The Macmillan Co., 1935), and *Myth, Ritual and Kingship: Essays on the Theory and Practice of Kingship in the Ancient Near East and in Israel* (Oxford: The Clarendon Press, 1958).

7. For descriptions of the "forms" found by form critics in the Old Testament, see Aage Bentzen, *Introduction to the Old Testament* (Copenhagen: G. E. C. Gad, 1957), I, 102-251; Artur Weiser, *The Old Testament; Its Formation and Development*, D. M. Barton, tr. (New York: Association Press, 1961), pp. 21-68; and O. Eissfeldt, *The Old Testament, an Introduction*, pp. 9-127. E. A. Leslie, *The Psalms, Translated and Interpreted in the Light of Hebrew Life and Worship* (Nashville: Abingdon Press, 1949), is an example of the use of form criticism in the study of the psalms.

8. There are a number of works available describing the contributions of archaeology to the study of the Old Testament. Pritchard, ed., *Ancient Near Eastern Texts* and *The Ancient Near East, an Anthology* provide important texts from the ancient Near East in English translation. These are what historians call "primary sources." For descriptive and interpretive surveys, see Jack Finegan, *Light from the Ancient Past, the Archaeological Background of Judaism and Christianity* (rev. ed.; Princeton: Princeton University Press, 1959), presenting archaeological finds in the framework of a conservative reconstruction of ancient history; John Gray, *Archaeology and the Old Testament World* (New York: Thomas Nelson & Sons, 1962), deals with archaeological data from the point of view of the History of Traditions School; G. E. Wright, *Biblical Archaeology* (Philadelphia: The Westminster Press, 1957), covers much of the same material as that reported in the other two works but from a third viewpoint. Seton Lloyd, *The Art of the Ancient Near East* (New York: Frederick A. Praeger, 1961), available also in paperback, will delight those who love art.

9. Oppenheim, "Babylonian and Assyrian Historical Texts," in Pritchard, ed., *Ancient Near Eastern Texts*, pp. 265-317, and *The Ancient Near East, an Anthology*, pp. 188-208. A more complete selection of Assyrian and Babylonian royal records is available in an older translation by D. D. Luckenbill, *Ancient Records of Assyria and Babylonia* (2 vols.; Chicago: University of Chicago Press, 1926, 1927).

10. The Hebrew Bible used for this was R. Kittel, ed., *Biblia Hebraica*, 3rd ed. rev. by A. Alt and O. Eissfeldt (Stuttgart: Privilegierte Württembergische Bibelanstalt, 1937). The Old Testament in English was the Oxford Annotated Bible. This table must be used with caution, and comparisons can only be made between the Hebrew text of one book and the Hebrew text of another—or the English text of one, and the English text of another. This preserves a uniformity of type and page size, as well as uniformity of language.

II

THE CANONICAL SAVING HISTORY

1

We will begin our study with the first six books of the Old Testament: Genesis, Exodus, Leviticus, Numbers, Deuteronomy, and Joshua. They are called the Hexateuch, a name formed from the two Greek words for "six books."

The Hexateuch opens with the creation of the world and of mankind—for which there are two stories: Genesis 1:1–2:4a, and 2:4b–3:24—and it closes with the division of Palestine among the twelve tribes of Israel and the death of Joshua, the leader of the invasion of Palestine (Josh. 13:8–24:33). It covers quite a lot of ground!

In Genesis we are told about the creation of the world and of all living beings, about the choice of the descendants of one man, Abraham, to become God's own people, and about the travels and slow growth of Abraham's family. By the end of Genesis, Abraham's grandson, Jacob, has twelve sons who are to become the "fathers" of the twelve tribes of Israel; and Jacob and his twelve sons have been driven into Egypt by famine in Palestine.

Exodus picks up the story after the children, grandchildren, and great-grandchildren of the twelve sons of Jacob have become twelve tribes. They are still in Egypt, but the pharaoh has enslaved them. A God who gives his name as Yahweh, the same God who had selected Abraham and his offspring to worship him, now picks a man named Moses to lead the enslaved Israelites out of Egypt into the desert to a holy mountain called Sinai, Horeb, or Seir. At the mountain, Moses and the Israelites see God come down the mountain:

(16) On the morning of the third day there were thunders and lightnings, and a thick cloud upon the mountain, and a very loud trumpet blast, so that all the people who were in the camp trembled.

(17) Then Moses brought the people out of the camp to meet God; and they took their stand at the foot of the mountain. (18) And Mount Sinai was wrapped in smoke, because the LORD descended upon it in fire; and the smoke of it went up like the smoke of a kiln, and the whole mountain quaked greatly. (19) And as the sound of the trumpet grew louder and louder, Moses spoke, and God answered him in thunder. (Ex. 19:16-19.)

Does this description remind you of anything else?

God and the people draw up an agreement called a covenant. God promises to accept this nation as his people and to take care of it as long as it obeys him. The people agree to worship only Yahweh and to do what he commands. One very old form of the agreement is described in Exodus 24:1-11. Another description of it comes near the end of the Hexateuch, after the Israelites are in Palestine (Josh. 24:1-27).

The laws, of which there are so many in the Hexateuch (about half of Exodus, all of Leviticus, part of Numbers, and most of Deuteronomy), are given to us as the rules God asks the Israelites to obey. Most of us learned the Ten Commandments as they are given in either Exodus 20:1-17 or Deuteronomy 5:6-21, but probably not as they appear in Exodus 34:17-28. These ten rules are only a small part of the laws of the Hexateuch, and scholars now believe that there are at least three different sets of laws, each with its own history: the Covenant Code (Ex. 20:22–23:33; 34) which the Israelites borrowed from the Canaanites, the people living in Palestine when the Israelites entered; the laws in Deuteronomy; and the Priestly Code made up of the balance of the laws in Exodus, Leviticus, and Numbers.

Many Christians find the stories in the Hexateuch fascinating, and there are some famous ones there: Adam and Eve in the Garden of Eden (Gen. 3), Noah's Ark (Gen. 6:11–9:17), the Tower of Babel (Gen. 11:1-9), the Destruction of Sodom and Gomorrah (Gen. 18:16–19:29), Jacob and Esau (Gen. 27:1-40), Rachel at the Well (Gen. 29:1-30), Joseph and the Coat of Many Colors (Gen. 37), the Infancy of Moses (Ex. 2:1-10), Moses and the Burning Bush (Ex. 3:1-22), the Golden Calf (Ex. 32), and many others.

Interest and value, however, are different matters. Christians have always enjoyed the stories of the Hexateuch, but they also have always tried to find meaning there. This has usually raised two problems: Are the laws of the Hexateuch still in force, or did they apply as the will of God only to the ancient Israelites? And, does the Hexateuch predict or foreshadow the coming of Christ? In general, Christians have been divided on the first but agreed on the second. Some Christians, like Martin Luther, have felt that the laws of the Old Testament have been repealed by the New Testament. Others, like John Calvin, have felt that a divine law is always in force. Everyone, however, has seen more or less clear hints of the coming of Christ.

Many Christians still debate these questions, but higher criticism has given an understanding of the Hexateuch which many scholars believe to be far closer to the original meaning than those just described. We are interested here in this newer view. To describe it, it is necessary to say something first about the history of the scholars' study of the Hexateuch.

Since modern scholarly study of the Hexateuch began in 1678, when Richard Simon, a Roman Catholic priest, published his *Histoire critique du Vieux Testament,* the story obviously is too long to be repeated in any detail here.[1] In brief, this is what happened:

Using literary criticism, scholars first discovered that there were four major sources in the Hexateuch, each of which had been edited at least once. Today, we call the four sources the Yahwist (because this author used Yahweh as the personal name of Israel's God in Genesis), the Elohist (because this writer used Elohim instead of Yahweh as the name for God in Genesis), the Deuteronomist (because the beginning of this source is the book of Deuteronomy), and the Priestly Document (because the authors of this showed a strong interest in the life and work of the priesthood).

Using historical criticism, scholars next learned that the age of these four sources in their final form is roughly as follows. The Yahwist and the Elohist are the oldest and may come from about 950 to 850 B.C., although these dates are far from certain. Deuteronomy was made the law of the land of Judah in 621 B.C. (it is believed to be the law code found by the priest Hilkiah, as reported in 2 Kings 22:3-13) and was probably written a few years earlier, perhaps about 650. It cannot have been too much earlier, however, because it was written in the style of the age of the prophet Jeremiah (626-586 B.C.). The Priestly Document was being written over a good many years and is to be dated in its final form after 500 B.C., probably closer to 400. These dates also are only approximate. What we are sure of is that the authors of the Yahwist and Elohist sources did not know many of the laws found in Deuteronomy, but the authors of the Priestly Document did. If we date Deuteronomy from 650 to 621 B.C., we conclude that the Yahwist and Elohist were written earlier than 650 to 621, and that the Priestly Document was later.[2]

Historical critics also discovered that the narratives in the Hexateuch had been passed down by word of mouth for centuries. Since historical criticism does not work very well with this kind of material, a strange problem arose. The various strata in the Hexateuch could be dated in relationship to each other, but it was impossible for historical critics to do very much about studying the events which may have been behind the stories in the strata. They had been passed down by word of mouth. This problem led to the discovery of form criticism, a tool for the study of materials with lengthy oral histories.

When form criticism was used in the Hexateuch, so much was learned that only a few of the general results can be described here. The first of these was that the sources already mentioned (the Yahwist, Elohist, Deuteronomist, and Priestly Document) were found to be collections of passages which originally had been independent of one another. This was so surprising that some scholars decided that the sources themselves had never really existed. Others continued to believe that there were sources such as the Yahwist, but they were convinced that the "authors" of these sources really were only editors. A third group of scholars came to believe that the authors of the sources were true authors, and that it was important to study the once independent passages and also the collecting of them into sources such as the Yahwist. One form of the third position is called the "History of Traditions School" and is the position which is followed here.[3]

2

The History of Traditions School sees the Hexateuch to be the end product of a gradual growth throughout much of Israelite history. Literary criticism is used to separate the sources in the Hexateuch. Form criticism is then used to break each source down into its parts, to discover how each part was used originally, and to try to date each part. Historical criticism is also used in dating individual stories, but it is needed chiefly to write the history of ancient Israel in the light of which the growing traditions of this people are to be understood.

We do all this each time we read a newspaper. As we go through it, hints in many articles tell us when and why they were written. We would know that a report of a speech on the Community Chest drive made before a service club was written after the address had been given if it included some of the questions asked by the audience. Most of us would link an industry announcement of a proposed price rise in aluminum with a rumor that the Federal Government was considering selling part of its defense stockpile of the metal, especially if we found another article reporting that "a highly placed" government official lamented inflationary trends in the economy. We have learned to understand the difference between a report of what someone said and a direct quotation of his words. In terms of the tools of research available for the study of the Bible, we are eclectics. We use several different tools while we read in order to increase our understanding of what we are reading. This is the way a scholar works who belongs to the History of Traditions School. He is an eclectic in methods, and he uses every tool of research available as it becomes useful.

He finds that there are several very old, short statements of what Yahweh did for Israel early in its history. One example is Deuteronomy 26:5-9:

(5) And you shall make response before the LORD your God, "A wandering Aramean was my father; and he went down into Egypt and sojourned there, few in number; and there he became a nation, great, mighty, and populous. (6) And the Egyptians treated us harshly, and afflicted us, and laid upon us hard bondage. (7) Then we cried to the LORD the God of our fathers, and the LORD heard our voice, and saw our affliction, our toil, and our oppression; (8) and the LORD brought us out of Egypt with a mighty hand and an outstretched arm, with great terror, with signs and wonders; (9) and he brought us into this place and gave us this land, a land flowing with milk and honey."

The first sentence makes it clear that this is part of an act of worship. Scholars call it a creed, or credo. There are few details given, just the bare outline of migration into Egypt, the enslavement there, deliverance, and entry into Palestine. Deuteronomy 6:20-24 is another brief creed, but compare Deuteronomy 26:5-9, given above, with Psalm 136:4-22:

> 4) To him who alone does great wonders,
>   for his steadfast love endures for ever;
> 5) to him who by understanding made the heavens,
>   for his steadfast love endures for ever;
> 6) to him who spread out the earth upon the waters,
>   for his steadfast love endures for ever;
> 7) to him who made the great lights,
>   for his steadfast love endures for ever;
> 8) the sun to rule over the day,
>   for his steadfast love endures for ever;
> 9) the moon and stars to rule over the night,
>   for his steadfast love endures for ever;

10) to him who smote the first-born of Egypt,
      for his steadfast love endures for ever;
11) and brought Israel out from among them,
      for his steadfast love endures for ever;
12) with a strong hand and an outstretched arm,
      for his steadfast love endures for ever;
13) to him who divided the Red Sea in sunder,
      for his steadfast love endures for ever;
14) and made Israel pass through the midst of it,
      for his steadfast love endures for ever;
15) but overthrew Pharaoh and his host in the Red Sea,
      for his steadfast love endures for ever;
16) to him who led his people through the wilderness,
      for his steadfast love endures for ever;
17) to him who smote great kings,
      for his steadfast love endures for ever;
18) and slew famous kings,
      for his steadfast love endures for ever;
19) Sihon, king of the Amorites,
      for his steadfast love endures for ever;
20) and Og, king of Bashan,
      for his steadfast love endures for ever;
21) and gave their land as a heritage,
      for his steadfast love endures for ever;
22) a heritage to Israel his servant,
      for his steadfast love endures for ever.

This psalm is a responsive reading and thus originally was part of a worship service. It expands the creed. Verses 4 through 9 add the creation, verse 10 describes one of the plagues in Egypt, verses 13 through 15 report the crossing of the Red Sea, verse 16 mentions the wandering in the wilderness, and verses 17 through 20 name kings defeated during the journey from Egypt to Canaan. Joshua 24:2-13 is another longer form of the recital.

The process of adding more and more events as the years passed is the way the Hexateuch, starting with a simple creed like Deuteronomy 26:5-9, finally grew into the six Old Testament books that now lie before you. But we should not try to trace any of the history of those additions until we understand somewhat how the minds of the people who made the expansion worked.

Very few people know how much they get from the culture in which they grow up. One of the benefits to be gained from living for a year in a foreign country is the discovery that the odd ways other people seem to have cease to be strange as they become familiar. All cultures are man-made, and all are learned. Anthropology is the attempt to describe the different ways people think and act in different cultures. These differences have been found to go so deep that each people believes that its ways of thinking and acting are right and that any other way is wrong. Thus we cannot understand what another people is saying or thinking if we do not know something about their culture, for they express themselves in the ways that seem right to them, not the ways that seem right to us. This is why we need to try to understand three features of the culture of the ancient Hebrews.

The first is the belief that the group is more important than the individual. This is very difficult for us to understand since we live in a culture in which the individual is all-important. Those of us, however, who remember the day on which the Second World War ended probably can recall an example of our being merged into the feeling of being primarily a part of a group. When we heard the news of the cessation of hostilities in the Pacific, we simply swarmed out into the streets to be together. It was only after the celebrating was hours old that we became individuals again. At first, we were merely Americans, a triumphant people.

The ancient Israelites defined the person as a part of a group. Judges 11:29-39 illustrates this. An ancient Israelite leader, Jephthah, swore to God that he would sacrifice "whoever comes forth from the doors of my house to meet me" if God would give him victory. He was victorious, and the story continues:

(34) Then Jephthah came to his home at Mizpah; and behold, his daughter came out to meet him with timbrels and with dances; she

was his only child; beside her he had neither son nor daughter. (35) And when he saw her, he rent his clothes, and said, "Alas, my daughter! You have brought me very low, and you have become the cause of great trouble to me; for I have opened my mouth to the LORD, and I cannot take back my vow." (36) And she said to him, "My father, if you have opened your mouth to the LORD, do to me according to what has gone forth from your mouth, now that the LORD has avenged you on your enemies, on the Ammonites." (37) And she said to her father, "Let this thing be done for me; let me alone two months, that I may go and wander on the mountains, and bewail my virginity, I and my companions." (38) And he said, "Go." And he sent her away for two months; and she departed, she and her companions, and bewailed her virginity upon the mountains. (39) At the end of two months, she returned to her father, who did with her according to his vow which he had made.

The girl did not say that her father had no right to sacrifice her. She simply mourned because she had not given birth to a son to strengthen her family. She lived in and through her family. She had no existence as an individual. In light of this, does the execution of all Achan's family for his sin become understandable (Josh. 7)?

What has just been described is sometimes called corporate solidarity.[4] It is important because it gives us one of the reasons for the growth of ancient Israel's traditions. The Hexateuch began as a short creed, like the one quoted earlier here, and grew into its present size. But why?

We can figure out for ourselves the first part of the answer. As a new group joined the nation, it brought along its own historical traditions. But it really did become part of the nation, and the nation really did absorb it. The history of the nation became the history of the new group, and the history of the new group was absorbed into the history of the nation. We have done this in the United States also. The early colonies were independent of one another, and even fought one another before the ratification of the Constitution. Each colony had its own history. Today, we are one nation. The history of each colony has become the history of the whole nation. It is my history, as an American, regardless of when my family actually came to this country.

This is what happened in ancient Israel. The small group that was the core of what was to become the Israelite nation had gone to Egypt, had been enslaved there, had been freed by Yahweh's power, and had come into Palestine. They were excited about the power and the goodness of Yahweh. Each time they joined with another tribe or clan, they told about the God that had helped them escape from Egypt and insisted that this God might be a good one to accept as the God of the alliance. The new tribe agreed, perhaps helped a bit in the decision by the military strength of the Yahwists. The ancient creed which once had belonged to one clan or tribe thus became the creed of more and more clans and tribes. But each tribe brought its own history along. It gave its history to the confederation, just as the confederation gave the new tribes the combined histories of all other members of the confederation.

We can trace some of these additions. Look back again at the two passages quoted earlier here, Deuteronomy 26:5-9 and Psalm 136:4-22. As was pointed out, the psalm has information not present in the short creed. It begins with creation, tells about one of the plagues in Egypt and the crossing of the Red Sea, and reports the defeat of two Amorite kings, Sihon and Og. The creation story has a complicated, independent history of its own. The plagues in Egypt and the crossing of the Red Sea are expansions of the original, brief account of the deliverance from Egypt. The defeat of Sihon and Og may have been chapters from once independent tribal histories.

Have you noticed that neither of these passages mentions Moses, Mount Sinai, the giving of the law, or says much about the years spent wandering in the wilderness? Deuteronomy 6:20-24—which is like Deuteronomy 26:5-9—and Joshua 24:1-13 do not emphasize these events either. If you were to read through the Hexateuch in one sitting, you would come away dazed but with the impression that Moses was the most important person in it, that the visit to Mount Sinai—or Mount Horeb, as it is called in Deuteronomy—was the most important event, and that the Israelites got all their laws there. Yet none of these is mentioned in the four early descriptions of the oldest chapters of Israel's history. Furthermore, if you looked outside the Hexateuch for references to Mount Sinai or to Moses, you would be startled. The name Sinai appears only four times elsewhere in the Old Testament (Judg. 5:5; Neh. 9:13; Ps. 68:8, 17). The name of Moses appears more often—sixty-two times—but half of these references are in four books produced by authors having the same point of view as the authors of the Priestly Document—who make much of Moses —and thus are late.

The best explanation yet found for these odd facts seems to be that the Moses stories, the meeting with God at Mount Sinai, the giving of the law at a holy mountain, and some of the events now included in the years of wandering in the wilderness happened originally to clans that became part of the Israelite people fairly late. The saving history had already taken form without these instances of God's intervention, and examples of the earlier version have survived in the Old Testament. The needs of later generations retelling the expanding epic also played a part in the shaping of the final form, as we will see in Section 3 of this chapter.

Additions to the early creed seem to have been made in accordance with two principles. The first has been described. A people that joined the nation accepted the history of the other tribes as its own history at the same time that it gave its own history to the rest of the nation. The second principle is the reason we have called the creed "the saving history" in the title of this chapter.

All sorts of things happened to these tribes, just as all sorts of things happen to any group of people. But all that they preserved out of this early period were memories of those events in which they felt that their God had acted. These events were so important that their group would have died had things turned out differently. Slaves who do not become free cease being a separate people. Nomads wandering in the desert die if they do not find water.

53

People who invade a country because they are starving in the desert either succeed or are destroyed. You can see a kind of "either/or" behind each story in the Hexateuch. Either it turns out well, or we die. The events that each group gave to the nation were the most important events of its history.

They were also the events over which the tribesmen rarely had much control. Few groups of slaves free themselves. Even starving men cannot make it rain in the desert. Small bands of nomads do not usually capture fortified cities and overthrow kingdoms. Yet each tribe came into the confederation with a report of an event out of its past when its existence hung in the balance. They felt that a god had saved them because they had known themselves to be helpless, yet they had survived. They were reporting a history of the acts by which they had been saved. It was salvation history. What happened, therefore, was that tribes which had joined the new nation agreed that the God who had saved them was Yahweh, the same God who had delivered one group from slavery in Egypt. As more and more groups joined the confederation, a longer and longer story of the salvation history of the tribes was told.

The framework of the salvation history was made up of five once separate themes which reported tersely parts from clan or tribal histories. The themes are: the exodus from Egypt, the entry into Palestine, the promise of a land to the fathers, wandering in the wilderness, and an appearance of God at a holy mountain. These themes were the skeleton, so to speak, of the expanding sacred history. The skeleton was then filled out with other stories which also once had an independent history. The plagues in Egypt, the celebration of the Passover, Moses striking the rock in the desert to get water, and events during the invasion are examples.[5]

As far as we can tell now, the expanding sacred history was repeated during a worship service held at regular intervals when the Israelites remembered and renewed the agreement with Yahweh upon which their federation with one another rested. A knowledge both of the structure of the agreement with Yahweh and of the festival commemorating it is important for understanding the Old Testament.

One of the many ways archaeology has helped the study of the Old Testament has been through the recovery of a knowledge of the kinds of covenant used in the ancient Near East. This happened when a group of treaties were found in the archives of the Hittite Empire dating from 1450 to 1200 B.C., roughly the time the Israelites were entering Palestine.

There were two kinds of contracts: those between equals and those between unequals. We will call the second type the royal covenant, since kings used it to confirm their power over subject peoples. Contracts, or covenants, between a god and a people were of the second kind. Royal covenants had six parts: (1) the introduction, in which the king was named and his greatness stated; (2) the historical summary, where the events in which the king had displayed his power over his future subjects were described; (3) the terms of the contract, the rules defining obedience established by the king; (4) the placement of the covenant, the name of the shrine where the covenant was to be kept and the times and places it was to be read; (5) the list of divine witnesses; (6) the means of enforcement, the curses that would follow disobedience to the covenant or the blessings that would come if the covenant were obeyed.[6]

All six parts of this royal covenant are present in the stories of the making of the covenant between Yahweh and Israel. Only one example of each part will be quoted here, but references to other examples of each stage will also be given.

1. *The Introduction:* And Joshua said to all the people, "Thus says the LORD, the God of Israel . . . (Josh. 24:2a; see also Ps. 136:1-3.)

2. *The Historical Summary:* (2b) 'Your fathers lived of old beyond the Euphrates, Terah, the father of Abraham and of Nahor; and they served other gods. (3) Then I took your father Abraham from beyond the River and led him through all the land of Canaan, and made his offspring many. I gave him Isaac; (4) and to Isaac I gave Jacob and

Esau. And I gave Esau the hill country of Seir to possess, but Jacob and his children went down to Egypt. (5) And I sent Moses and Aaron, and I plagued Egypt with what I did in the midst of it; and afterwards I brought you out. (6) Then I brought your fathers out of Egypt, and you came to the sea; and the Egyptians pursued your fathers with chariots and horsemen to the Red Sea. (7) And when they cried to the LORD, he put darkness between you and the Egyptians, and made the sea come upon them and cover them; and your eyes saw what I did to Egypt; and you lived in the wilderness a long time. (8) Then I brought you to the land of the Amorites, who lived on the other side of the Jordan; they fought with you, and I gave them into your hand, and you took possession of their land, and I destroyed them before you. (9) Then Balak the son of Zippor, king of Moab, arose and fought against Israel; and he sent and invited Balaam the son of Beor to curse you, (10) but I would not listen to Balaam; therefore he blessed you; so I delivered you out of his hand. (11) And you went over the Jordan and came to Jericho, and the men of Jericho fought against you, and also the Amorites, the Perizzites, the Canaanites, the Hittites, the Girgashites, the Hivites, and the Jebusites; and I gave them into your hand. (12) And I sent the hornet before you, which drove them out before you, the two kings of the Amorites; it was not by your sword or by your bow. (13) I gave you a land on which you had not labored, and cities which you had not built, and you dwell therein; you eat the fruit of vineyards and oliveyards which you did not plant.' (Josh. 24:2b-13; see also Deut. 6:21-23; 26:5-9; Ps. 136:4-22.)

3. *The Terms of the Contract:* (14) "Now therefore fear the LORD, and serve him in sincerity and in faithfulness; put away the gods which your fathers served beyond the River, and in Egypt, and serve the LORD. (15) And if you be unwilling to serve the LORD, choose this day whom you will serve, whether the gods your fathers served in the region beyond the River, or the gods of the Amorites in whose land you dwell; but as for me and my house, we will serve the LORD." (Josh. 24:14-15; see Deut. 6:24-25; 5:6-21.)

4. *The Placement of the Contract:* And Joshua wrote these words in the book of the law of God; and he took a great stone, and set it up there under the oak in the sanctuary of the LORD. (Josh. 24:26.)

5. *The List of Witnesses:* (22) Then Joshua said to the people, "You are witnesses against yourselves that you have chosen the Lord, to serve him." And they said, "We are witnesses." ... (27) And Joshua said to all the people, "Behold, this stone shall be a witness against us; for it has heard all the words of the Lord which he spoke to us; therefore it shall be a witness against you, lest you deal falsely with your God." (Josh. 24:22, 27.)

6. *The Blessings and Curses:* (10) "You shall therefore obey the voice of the Lord your God, keeping his commandments and his statutes, which I command you this day." (11) And Moses charged the people the same day, saying, (12) "When you have passed over the Jordan, these shall stand upon Mount Gerizim to bless the people: Simeon, Levi, Judah, Issachar, Joseph, and Benjamin. (13) And these shall stand upon Mount Ebal for the curse: Reuben, Gad, Asher, Zebulun, Dan, and Naphtali." (Deut. 27:10-13; see also Deut. 11:30-35; Josh. 8:30-35.)

Five of the six stages were quoted from Joshua 24, a passage which describes a covenant between God and Israel made under Joshua's leadership at Shechem. The sixth stage was quoted from Deuteronomy 27. When we learn that Shechem was in the valley between Mount Ebal and Mount Gerizim, it becomes clear that the three passages reporting curses and blessings (Deut. 27:10-13; 11:30-35; Josh. 8:30-35) were laid originally at Shechem. Thus all the parts of the royal covenant are present in these descriptions of the rite practiced at Shechem. Is it reasonable to conclude, therefore, that the Shechem rite was the one in which the ancient saving history took shape?

3

This was the state of affairs before the first stratum, the Yahwist, was written: the Israelites not only had their independent tribal traditions, they also had a body of unified tradition which had come into being as a part of a rite of covenant renewal held at

Shechem. The next stage in the growth of the Hexateuch is the writing of the Yahwist source. Before we see what its author did, we need to try to understand two other things about the culture in which the authors of the Old Testament lived. The first is their idea of the past.

We think of the past as something that happened before the present. It is ended, finished. The Israelites saw the matter differently. The past was something which both happened "way back then" and continued to happen in the present time. This really does seem to be the way it is. The rails of standard gauge railroad track are just as far apart as were the wheels of the chariots of the ancient Romans, even though a wider gauge gives a smoother ride and a narrower gauge is cheaper to construct! We say that the sun rises in the morning and sets in the evening, and that we fly to the four corners of the earth; yet these are ways of speaking inherited from a picture of the universe which educated people have rejected for centuries. Almost everything we do and believe comes to us from the past, and the past lives on in us. The new often is only a slight change in the old.

The Israelites had a dynamic view of the past and tried constantly to make their memory of the past fully a part of their lives in the present. They retold the story of the past in terms of their current understanding.[7] Something would happen today which would make them see yesterday in a new light. We also do this. A history of the First World War written in 1920 differs sharply from one written in 1962!

A tremendous change took place in Israelite life about 1000 B.C. A people which had once been nomadic and had been ruled by the older men in the clans and tribes accepted a king. It is hard for us to understand fully all that this meant to them, but one part of it is clear. Earlier in their history, they had had so little organization that they threatened no one else. They had invaded Palestine by moving into the hills where no one else lived. Only rarely did they capture cities, as one frank description of their entry admits.

(29) And Ephraim did not drive out the Canaanites who dwelt in Gezer; but the Canaanites dwelt in Gezer among them. (30) Zebulun did not drive out the inhabitants of Kitron, or the inhabitants of Nahalol; but the Canaanites dwelt among them, and became subject to forced labor. (31) Asher did not drive out the inhabitants of Acco, or the inhabitants of Sidon, or of Ahlab, or of Achzib, or of Helbah, or of Aphik, or of Rehob; (32) but the Asherites dwelt among the Canaanites, the inhabitants of the land; for they did not drive them out. (Judg. 1:27-36; vss. 29-32 quoted.)

The comment that the Canaanites became subject to forced labor —something to which the Israelites also were subject during the reign of Solomon—meant that they were forced to work a specified number of days for the king each year without pay (see 1 Kings 5:13-16; 11:28; 12:4, 14-16). The Israelite tribes before the time of David were so disorganized and so weak that their lack of power was their defense. The crises in their history—when God needed to intervene—all had been in the distant past. Thus their salvation history spoke only of far-distant events, the exceptional crisis, and reported divine intervention accomplished in wonderful ways.

As soon as they acquired a king, he established an army, captured cities, and collected tribute. The Israelite monarchy became a threat to Israel's neighbors, and Israel's continued existence was always in danger. Now the Israelites needed to discover whether or not God was constantly active, protecting them from their enemies. They needed a knowledge of how he directed their daily living and how he protected them daily. The author of the Yahwist source was convinced that he could answer both questions, and he retold the ancient salvation history as his way of giving his answers.

We need one more bit of information. If I asked you what a chair is, you could tell me that it is something that holds me up off the floor when I sit, that it is something on which I sit, or that it is a movable seat with four legs and a back. If you study these definitions, you will discover that the first defines the chair by what it does, the second by how I use it, and the third by its traits, its essence. The first and the second are almost the same.

59

Both depend upon activity or use, and they differ only in terms of the subject of the action. The chair itself is the subject of the first definition; the user is the subject of the second definition. Thus, a chair is either something which pushes me up from the floor, or it is a tool I use for sitting. But the third definition differs from the other two. It does not discuss what happens. It talks about those parts of an object, which we call a chair, that must always be present if there be a chair present. We tend today to prefer the precision of the third kind of definition. It helps us to distinguish between a chair and a stool. The ancient Israelites, however, preferred a different kind of precision. They wanted to know exactly who used the seat.

We want to know what God is. The ancient Israelites wanted to know what God was doing. We say that God is love. The Israelites spoke of God loving. The result of this is that the ancient Israelite would often try to describe what we call a truth in terms of how the truth worked. He would tell or retell a story. He would tell or retell an event. This is what the Yahwist did. He had a new understanding of how God disclosed himself to men, of how God was acting in the nation's history. He did not state this as a series of abstract ideas. He retold the ancient salvation history.

The Yahwist (J)

Now for the strata of the Hexateuch. The oldest is the Yahwist. This author lived early in the monarchy and wanted to describe how God acted in current events by influencing the minds and wills of men. In order to explain this to himself and to others, the Yahwist retold the ancient salvation history which had come into existence as the nation had come into being.

He began at the very beginning and reported one of the stories of creation (Gen. 2:4b–3:24). He then set the stage for the birth of the Israelite people by reporting how God tried twice to get all men to serve him. The first attempt ended with the flood (Gen.

6:1-8; 7:1-8: 22, mixed in with P), the second with the building of the Tower of Babel (Gen. 11:1-9). Yahweh then decided to make a third attempt working with only one nation. He started with one man, Abraham (or Abram), who had to be persuaded to leave home and to move to the land of promise (Gen. 12:1-4). The plan almost failed several times. Abraham had no children. How could he sire a great nation? Yahweh promised a son (Gen. 18:1-15. Notice that the divine visitor is sometimes one man, sometimes three. There may have been two ancient stories of this which the Yahwist merged.) The son then needed a wife, and a servant goes back to Abraham's home to get one. So it goes. Yahweh's will is always worked out through men whom he guides and inspires. This, plus the desire to praise the monarchy established by David, is the purpose for the Yahwist's retelling of the salvation history.

THE ELOHIST (E)

The second retelling, the Elohist, is so much like the Yahwist that we will not stop here to discuss it. It seems to have come into existence when the kingdom founded by David broke apart into two smaller kingdoms after the death of Solomon, David's son. The kings who ruled in Jerusalem had the Yahwist as their royal history, but the kings of the new northern kingdom needed their own account of the past. The work of the Elohist seems to have been their history.

DEUTERONOMY (D)

The third major stratum of the Hexateuch is Deuteronomy. This is quite different from the Yahwist and the Elohist. Part of the reason is that the Deuteronomic School retold the salvation history for a different reason. The members of this group began to work about 650 B.C. Both the Yahwist and the Elohist wrote when the present and the future of the nation seemed promising. The nation was strong, and it might become stronger. The Deuteronomic School came into existence near the end of a century of foreign rule, when it seemed possible that the Assyrian Empire, which had enslaved Judah, might collapse. The Yahwist wanted to explain both how Yahweh revealed himself to men in daily life and why he was rewarding the Israelites by independence and prosperity. The Deuteronomic School wanted to help free Israel from its bondage to Assyria by reviving and modernizing the ancient covenant festival which once had told of Yahweh's liberation of Israel from bondage in Egypt. Thus the Deuteronomic School retold history for a quite different reason from the one that had motivated the Yahwist.

But the Deuteronomic School retold only a part of the salvation history. The main body of the book of Deuteronomy, which is chiefly law and preaching, was given a narrative framework. Deuteronomy 1–3 tells of the journey under Moses from Mount Horeb—the name for the holy mountain used by the Deuteronomic School—to the plains of Moab, just east of Palestine. The Deuteronomists may have accepted the telling of the earlier parts of the saving history by either the Yahwist or the Elohist. The next chapter of Deuteronomy is a retelling of the making of the agreement between Yahweh and Israel at the holy mountain. Deuteronomy 5–30 stresses the terms of the agreement between Yahweh and Israel, although there are bits of narrative and sermons here also. Deuteronomy 31; 32:44-52; 34 are the conclusion and tell of the final days of Moses' life, his death and burial. Chapter 32:1-43 is a hymn. Chapter 33 is an ancient, poetic description of the Israelite tribes.

If you leaf through Deuteronomy 5–30, you will find several kinds of material. The Ten Commandments appear here (Deut. 5:6-21), as does an old form of the ancient creed with which we began our description of the Hexateuch (Deut. 26:5-9). The contents of some of the chapters seem to be sermonic, such as Deuteronomy 6:10-15:

(10) And when the LORD your God brings you into the land which he swore to your fathers, to Abraham, to Isaac, and to Jacob, to give you, with great and goodly cities, which you did not build, (11) and houses full of all good things, which you did not fill, and cisterns hewn out, which you did not hew, and vineyards and olive trees, which you did not plant, and when you eat and are full, (12) then take heed lest you forget the LORD, who brought you out of the land of Egypt, out of the house of bondage. (Vss. 10-12 quoted.)

Deuteronomy 27:15-25 is a reminder of the importance of the royal covenant in the minds of the authors of Deuteronomy. It reports the curses that were to befall a people that disobeyed its covenant with God.

There are also laws which cover all sorts of things, such as special holy days (Deut. 16:13-15), the treatment of animals (Deut. 25:4, a passage which Paul used quite differently later), rules for warfare (Deut. 20:10-20), and rules governing weights and measures (Deut. 25:13-16). Anyone who has ever felt the breath of a draft board on his neck will find Deuteronomy 20:5-7 interesting.

(5) Then the officers shall speak to the people, saying, "What man is there that has built a new house and has not dedicated it? Let him go back to his house, lest he die in the battle and another man dedicate it. (6) And what man is there that has planted a vineyard and has not enjoyed its fruit? Let him go back to his house, lest he die in the battle and another man enjoy its fruit. (7) And what man is there that has betrothed a wife and has not taken her? Let him go back to his house, lest he die in the battle and another man take her."

Such an addition to our selective service act might guarantee a constant boom in building and viticulture! The authors of these laws seem to have known about the laws now found in Exodus 20:22–23:19; 34, but they ignored many of the laws found elsewhere in the Hexateuch. Does this mean that these passages in Exodus were earlier than Deuteronomy, but that the other laws were later?

If you would like to attempt some historical criticism, read 2 Kings 23:4-24 carefully. This is a description of the reformation carried out by King Josiah in Jerusalem in 621 B.C. Write out everything that King Josiah did, and then try to find the laws in the Hexateuch which command each of these acts. In some cases you will find several laws in different parts of the Hexateuch which apply. But if you find only one part—such as Deuteronomy —which orders done everything that Josiah did, have you found the law code by which he was governed in carrying out his reformation? This experiment was first proposed in 1806 by a Dutch scholar, Wilhelm DeWette, who concluded that Josiah's law book was the code of the book of Deuteronomy. If this is right—and you can test it for yourself—can we fit Deuteronomy into the history of salvation we have been studying?

It was suggested that Deuteronomy was the attempt to revive and to revise a special act of worship, the reliving of the acts of Yahweh out of which Israel as a people had been born. This festival has also been called the covenant renewal festival, since the covenant originally arose as a result of the belief in God's saving acts. It would be most properly renewed by reliving those same saving acts.

Here are some of reasons for believing this. First, the part of the salvation history which the Deuteronomic writers retold most fully is the covenant-making at Horeb. This is why most of the book is law, and pleas to obey the law. Second, the oldest fragments of the covenant-making ceremony to have survived are found in Deuteronomy (26:5-9; 6:20-24; 27:11-26). Third, the contents of the book as a whole were put in the form of a covenant renewal festival: a description of the mighty acts through which God proclaimed himself to be Israel's God; a listing of some of the laws which Israel accepted as its duty under the agreement; a list of curses and blessings intended to help enforce the covenant; and sermons urging the people to obey the agreement.

This suggestion also makes sense if we study Deuteronomy in terms of Israelite history. The original agreement-making festival started when a clan or tribe celebrated its escape from Egypt. For more than a century (since 734 B.C.), the royal chapel in Jerusalem had been used for the worship of Ashur, the god of Assyria (see 2 Kings 16:1-16). During this time, Judah had paid a very heavy tribute to Assyria. Farsighted men suspected that collapse of Assyria was near and hoped that it might happen in such a way that Judah could become free again. This would be another mighty, saving act by Yahweh since Judah could not free itself by its own strength. Some Israelites thought that reviving the ancient agreement-making ceremony might encourage Yahweh to act on behalf of his people, leading them into independence and prosperity once more. So understood, Deuteronomy becomes another retelling of the past because of a present need.

THE PRIESTLY DOCUMENT (P)

The fourth great stratum in the Hexateuch is called the Priestly Document, or Code. It, like the Yahwist, starts at creation and goes through to the invasion of Palestine, although it often provides little more than a framework in which earlier sources carry the story. Genesis 1:1–2:4a is the Priestly story of creation, and it is interesting to compare this with the older Yahwist story in Genesis 2:4b–3:24, as well as with the Enuma Elish, the Babylonian creation story.[8] The Priestly account of the invasion is told in Joshua (along with material from other sources). The Priestly Code has some things the other strata lack, such as an interest in family histories. If you like tongue twisters, try reading this aloud.

(1) These are the generations of the sons of Noah, Shem, Ham, and Japheth; sons were born to them after the flood. (2) The sons of Japheth: Gomer, Magog, Madai, Javan, Tubal, Meshech, and Tiras. (3) The sons of Gomer: Ashkenaz, Riphath, and Togarmah. (4) The sons of Javan: Elishah, Tarshish, Kittim, and Dodanim. (5) From these the coastland peoples spread. These are the sons of Japheth in their lands, each with his own language, by their families, in their nations. (Gen. 10:1-5; see also vss. 6-32.)

Other examples of this genealogical interest can be found in Genesis 5:1-32 and 11:10-32. But are these genealogies, or are they tables of nations?

The main interest of the authors of this stratum was making long lists of laws to govern all of ancient Israel's life. They described how a movable shrine should be built, how priests should marry and whom they could marry, what Israelites could eat and wear, and how to punish a dangerous ox. You will find part of their laws in Leviticus, and more in Exodus and Numbers. It is fascinating to read through Leviticus making a list of the subjects covered. There are some odd ones!

If you do this, and if you remember that scholars date the Priestly Source after the destruction of the Israelite kingdoms, you will discover for yourself why scholars believe this stratum in the Hexateuch to be the final retelling of the salvation history. Once again, there was a new need. The early forms of the saving history came into being as the nation was being born. The Yahwist and Elohist retold it in response to the creation of the monarchy. The Deuteronomic School retold it in response to the approaching end of the Assyrian Empire. The Priestly School retold it all once more as its attempt to restore the nation as an institution ruled by priests, after the exile had marked the end of the monarchy. Thus the Priestly Source is a bit like the Constitution of the United States, except that it is the constitution of an ecclesiastical organization which was also to serve as the civil government.

We call the saving history that was told and retold so many times "the canonical saving history." "Canonical" means authoritative, and it must have been authoritative for ancient Israel or it would not have been retold so often and so carefully.

4

What does the view of the Hexateuch given here mean for us? It does not predict the coming of Christ, and it should not be used as a source for rules of modern morality. The rules, or laws, in the

Hexateuch were the laws governing an ancient nation to which we do not belong.

It is neither possible nor desirable to list here all the meaning of this view of the Hexateuch. Meaning is always more important when we discover it for ourselves, but some hints can be given here. These hints may stimulate your mind.

The first hint is that seeing the Hexateuch as it has been described here frees us to look in it for insights Christians could not find earlier because they were looking for something else. Here is an example.

The creation story in the Priestly Document tells us how God brought order out of chaos (Gen. 1:1–2:4a). It also tells us that we are created in God's image (Gen. 1:26-27). Does this mean that being like God is at least partly the ability to bring order out of chaos? If this be so, then how important are such everyday experiences as cleaning a house or organizing a job? Morality is partly a matter of bringing order into a disordered life and into disordered relations between people. Does morality become important in the light of this view of the meaning of Genesis 1? What about scholarship, which is the attempt to bring order into our knowledge of ourselves and our world.

The second hint is that the view of the growth of the Hexateuch described here is—if it be correct—also a description of an important part of the life of the ancient Israelite "church." Remembering the past actions of God in such a way that we are able to see him acting in the present thus becomes very important in any true "biblical faith." What would this mean for your faith? Does it have any significance for the life of the church today?

NOTES

1. A brief history of scholarly interpretation of the Bible is given by Samuel Terrien in "History of the Interpretation of the Bible: Modern Period," *The Interpreter's Bible*, ed. G. A. Buttrick, *et al.* (Nashville: Abingdon Press, 1952), I, 127-41. The most comprehensive review of the history

of the subject is Hans-Joachim Kraus, *Geschichte der historisch-kritischen Erforschung des Alten Testament von der Reformation bis zur Gegenwart* (Neukirchen, Kreis Moers: Buchhandlung des Erziehungsvereins, 1956).

2. For an older treatment of the matter, see Julius K. Bewer, *The Literature of the Old Testament* (3rd ed., New York: Columbia University Press, [1933] 1962), as follows: for the Yahwist (J), pp. 60-73; for the Elohist (E), pp. 74-86; for Deuteronomy (D), pp. 121-35; for the Priestly Source (P), pp. 259-79. For a more recent statement, see Norman K. Gottwald, *A Light to the Nations: An Introduction to the Old Testament* (New York: Harper & Row, 1959), as follows: for the Yahwist, pp. 214-33; for the Elohist, pp. 246-54; for Deuteronomy, pp. 334-46; and for the Priestly Source, pp. 448-68.

3. For an early—yet still basic—statement of the History of Traditions School's analysis of the Hexateuch, see Gerhard von Rad, "The Form-critical Problem of the Hexateuch," in *The Problem of the Hexateuch and Other Essays*, E. W. Trueman Dicken, tr. (New York: McGraw-Hill Book Company, 1966), pp. 1-78. A more detailed History of Traditions study of the first five books of the Old Testament is available in Martin Noth, *Überlieferungsgeschichte des Pentateuch* (Stuttgart: W. Kohlhammer, 1948).

4. For more complete descriptions of this, see H. Wheeler Robinson, "The Hebrew Conception of Corporate Personality," in *Werden und Wesen des Alten Testaments*, ed. P. Volz, F. Stummer, and J. Hempel (Berlin: Alfred Töpelmann, 1936), pp. 49-62; and—using the term "psychic wholeness,"—Johs. Pedersen, *Israel, Its Life and Culture* (Copenhagen: Povl Branner, [1926] 1946), Pts. I-II, pp. 99-181.

5. This list of the major component parts of the saving history is taken from Noth, *Überlieferungsgeschichte des Pentateuch.*

6. Discussed by George E. Mendenhall, *Law and Covenant in Israel and the Ancient Near East* (Pittsburgh: The Biblical Colloquium, 1955), a reprint of two articles, the second of which is the more important for us: "Covenant Forms in Israelite Tradition," *Biblical Archaeologist*, XVII, 1954, pp. 50-76. A much fuller treatment of the matter is provided in Dennis J. McCarthy, S.J., *Treaty and Covenant* ([Analecta Biblica No. 21] Rome: Pontifical Biblical Institute, 1963), pp. 181-205, where translations of the ancient royal treaties being discussed are also provided.

7. For an expanded discussion of this see Gerhard von Rad, *Old Testament Theology, The Theology of Israel's Historical Traditions*, O. M. G. Stalker, tr. (New York: Harper & Row, 1962), I, 105-305.

8. E. A. Speiser, "Akkadian Myths and Epics," in Pritchard, ed., *Ancient Near Eastern Texts*, pp. 60-72; and *The Ancient Near East: An Anthology*, pp. 31-86.

III

THE DEUTERONOMIC HISTORY

1

Five of the ten books of history in the Old Testament display such similarities in style that many biblical scholars think of them as a single historical work. These are Judges, 1 and 2 Samuel, and 1 and 2 Kings.[1] Since the authors of this history made extensive use of earlier sources—many of which they seem to have quoted— their own style is to be found in their editorial framework for the earlier sources. This editorial material has so many similarities of style and content with Deuteronomy that Judges, 1 and 2 Samuel, and 1 and 2 Kings are called the Deuteronomic History. Thus the Deuteronomic Code (the book of Deuteronomy) and the Deuteronomic History together make up the Deuteronomic Work.[2] All six books reflect the work of a single school active over a number of years, and a single point of view dominates all six books.

The reasons for dating the book of Deuteronomy at about 650 B.C. were given in the last chapter. If we assume that the Deuteronomic historians worked at least as late as the last event reported in their history, we arrive at a date of about 560 B.C. for the close of their activity. 2 Kings 25:27-30 reports that Jehoiachin, deposed and imprisoned by the Babylonians in 598 B.C., was freed by Evil-merodach (Awil-Marduk) when that Babylonian king came to his throne in 560 B.C. The biblical passage also dates the event in the seventeenth year of Jehoiachin's captivity. Since Jehoiachin became a royal prisoner in 598, his release would have taken place in 561 or 560. The two methods for dating given us in 2 Kings 25:27-30 yield the same result, and we can date the last event reported by the Deuteronomic History in 560.[3] Thus it is possible that the Deuteronomic School was active from 650 to 560 B.C.

The Deuteronomic School worked during a chaotic century. The school began shortly after Esarhaddon (681-665) extended Assyrian rule to Egypt. It witnessed the swift disintegration of the Assyrian Empire and shared in the brief moment of Judaean independence under Josiah (621-609), when the Deuteronomic Code became the basis of a new covenant between the nation and its God. Members of the school witnessed Josiah's death in battle in 609, shared in the humiliation of the Egyptian and the Babylonian conquests, and saw Jerusalem captured in 598 and again in 586 B.C. The final chapters of the history, as well as the last editorial revisions throughout the Deuteronomic work, seem to have been added during the Exile.

2

The Deuteronomic History can be broken down into its component parts either in terms of its sources or its chronological divisions.

A. *Modern Old Testament scholars have found it profitable to uncover the sources used by these historians.* If we wish to rewrite the history of ancient Israel in order to include information from nonbiblical sources given us by archaeologists, we need to be able to identify and to evaluate the different materials used in writing the Deuteronomic History. The editorial framework is commentary, not reporting of events. Royal annals—precise records of events kept by court officials—were more accurate than were popular legends. Thus the uncovering and the historical evaluation of the sources in the Deuteronomic History is the first step in using these Old Testament books to write a modern history of the Israelite monarchy.

But we also need to identify the Deuteronomic historians' sources before we can study their thought. If we can compare that which they reported from their sources with that which they ignored in those same sources, we can begin to see their value judgments at work; and when we can distinguish between a source they quoted and something they themselves wrote, we can isolate their own statements for study. The Deuteronomic History is as important to us as a theology as it is as a history—perhaps more important—and we should study it in ways which make it possible for us to recover the theology.

The sources used are quite varied and seem to contradict one another at times. A tribal legend about the rise of Saul to the throne which seems quite historical (1 Sam. 11) was merged with a nonhistorical popular legend glorifying Samuel (1 Sam. 9:1–10: 16). A long, nearly self-contained epic about the rise of David to the throne (1 Sam. 16:14–2 Sam. 5:12) now stands side by side with the somber story of David's adultery with Bathsheba and its deadly aftermath (2 Sam. 11:1–18:33). A precise, impartial description of King Hezekiah's defeat (2 Kings 18:13-16) follows a Deuteronomic editorial summary which asserts that Yahweh was with Hezekiah in all that he did (2 Kings 18:3-8). A brief, favorable summary of the reign of Jeroboam II (2 Kings 14:25-26) is now embedded in a hostile Deuteronomic editorial framework (2 Kings 14:23-24, 28-29).

One classification of the kinds of materials used in 1 and 2 Kings lists royal archives (called the Chronicles of the Kings of Judah and the Chronicles of the Kings of Israel), records of specific military campaigns (such as those mentioned in 1 Kings 14:19, 30; 2 Kings 14:15), Temple archives (such as the description of the interior of the Temple in 1 Kings 7:15-50), histories of political crises (such as the story of Absalom's revolt in 2 Sam. 15:1–18:33), and legends about individual prophets (of which the Elijah cycle in 1 Kings 17–19 and 21, 2 Kings 2; and the Elisha cycle chiefly in 2 Kings 2–9 are the best known).[4] If we include in our review of the Deuteronomists' sources those used in Judges and 1 Samuel, we add early tribal histories, sagas of intertribal cooperation (such as Judg. 5), and sanctuary legends (such as the story of the boy Samuel in the sanctuary at Shiloh in 1 Sam. 3).

B. *The other way to divide the Deuteronomic History is by its chronological units:* (a) the period of the judges (Judg. 2–1 Sam. 7); (b) the period of the united monarchy (1 Sam. 8–1 Kings 11); and (c) the period of the divided monarchy (1 Kings 12–2 Kings 25). Each of these periods can be further subdivided. The united monarchy lasted through the reigns of Saul, David, and Solomon, for example. Nevertheless, we will need only the threefold division just proposed.

The period of the judges describes the life of Israel during the age of the tribal confederation when each tribe had its own leader. At times, several of the tribes rallied under a single leader, and Judges 5 sings of such an hour. Verses 13 to 18 name the tribes involved.

> 13) Then down marched the remnant of the noble;
>   the people of the LORD marched down for him
>   against the mighty.
> 14) From Ephraim they set out thither into the valley,
>   following you, Benjamin, with your kinsmen;
>   from Machir marched down the commanders,
>   and from Zebulun those who bear the marshal's staff;
> 15) the princes of Issachar came with Deborah,
>   and Issachar faithful to Barak;
>   into the valley they rushed forth at his heels.
>   Among the clans of Reuben
>   there were great searchings of heart.
> 16) Why did you tarry among the sheepfolds,
>   to hear the piping for the flocks?
>   Among the clans of Reuben
>   there were great searchings of heart.
> 17) Gilead stayed beyond the Jordan;
>   and Dan, why did he abide with the ships?
>   Asher sat still at the coast of the sea,
>   settling down by his landings.
> 18) Zebulun is a people that jeopardied their lives

to the death;
Naphtali too, on the heights of the field.

At other times, the tribes fought alone. Occasionally, at least, they fought one another. Jephthah led Gilead into battle against the non-Israelite Ammonites, but he finished the campaign by fighting against the Israelite Ephraimites (Judg. 11:4–12:6); and "all Israel" nearly destroyed the tribe of Benjamin (Judg. 20).

This part of the Deuteronomic History was given its present form by the Deuteronomic historians. They merged independent tribal histories—which originally covered the same period of time—into a national history and transformed each tribal leader into a "judge" of all Israel. The newly formed epic was held together by an editorial framework which expressed a theological judgment in the form of a narrative formula. The narrative formula appears first in Judges 2:11-16.

(11) And the people of Israel did what was evil in the sight of the LORD and served the Baals; (12) and they forsook the LORD, the God of their fathers, who had brought them out of the land of Egypt; they went after other gods, from among the gods of the peoples who were round about them, and bowed down to them; and they provoked the LORD to anger. (13) They forsook the LORD, and served the Baals and the Ashtaroth. (14) So the anger of the LORD was kindled against Israel, and he gave them over to plunderers, who plundered them; and he sold them into the power of their enemies round about, so that they could not longer withstand their enemies. (15) Whenever they marched out, the hand of the LORD was against them for evil, as the LORD had warned, and as the LORD had sworn to them; and they were in sore straits. (16) Then the LORD raised up judges, who saved them out of the power of those who plundered them.

Then a new cycle of faithlessness began. This editorial framework appears again and again in the book of Judges. (See, for examples, Judg. 3:7-11; 10:6-16.)

Two features of the Deuteronomic framework are particularly

noteworthy. The first is the appearance of a brief recapitulation of the creed which served as the basis for the Shechemite covenant renewal festival and which the Deuteronomic law givers also preserved in the Deuteronomic Code.

(7) When the people of Israel cried to the LORD on account of the Midianites, (8) the LORD sent a prophet to the people of Israel; and he said to them, "Thus says the LORD, the God of Israel; I led you up from Egypt, and brought you out of the house of bondage; (9) and I delivered you from the hand of the Egyptians, and from the hand of all who oppressed you, and drove them out before you, and gave you their land; (10) and I said to you, 'I am the LORD your God; you shall not pay reverence to the gods of the Amorites, in whose land you dwell.' But you have not given heed to my voice." (Judg. 6:7-10; see also Judg. 10:11-14; compare with Deut. 6:20-25; 26:5-9.)

A second notable feature of the Deuteronomic framework is the nature of the leadership through which God acted to help his people. Each leader was "raised up" specifically for the act of salvation done through him. We are given a description later of a moment in Saul's life when he was raised up to rescue the men of Jabesh-Gilead from the Ammonites. Messengers from Jabesh seeking Israelite help for their besieged village came to Saul's village just before he returned from the fields in the evening.

(5) Now Saul was coming from the field behind the oxen; and Saul said, "What ails the people, that they are weeping?" So they told him the tidings of the men of Jabesh. (6) And the spirit of God came mightily upon Saul when he heard these words, and his anger was greatly kindled. (1 Sam. 11:5-6.)

But the charisma of God not only produced a vast anger in Saul, it also gave him the ability to lead men. He rallied the Israelites and led them to relieve Jabesh-Gilead.

"Charisma" means "a free gift from God." Here, the gift is the transformation of a man by the spirit of God. The judges were leaders because they were believed to be filled with the spirit of God. One need only listen to a modern congregation drone slowly through a hymn such as "Spirit of God, Descend upon My Heart" to suspect that this is not precisely the kind of divine spirit that so enraged Saul that his fury goaded a whole nation into action. For the ancient Israelite, God's spirit was his power.[5] For the spiritual person to be quiet and passive would have been taken as an indication that the God who had given his spirit was powerless. Great men in Israel were greater than their fellows because the Lord had endowed them with an unusual measure of his spirit. A charismatic leader was a person of exceptional abilities, but his leadership was limited to the crisis for which Yahweh had raised him up. Israel had betrayed its agreement with God, and God had punished Israel by abandoning it to its enemies. The punishment brought Israel to its senses, and it cried unto the Lord. God then aroused a judge through whom he freed Israel from its oppressor.

Thus the Deuteronomic editorial framework for the period of the judges pictures Yahweh as bringing upon Israel the blessings or the curses of the royal covenant. Because God had freed this people from Egypt and had brought it to the land of Canaan, it should serve him faithfully. When it refused to serve him but served other gods, he punished it. Israel then repented, turned again to Yahweh, and promised fervently to serve him. This was faithfulness, and he responded, acting through a leader chosen for this one moment. The editorial framework always adds that Israel, released from the curse, turned away again. For the Deuteronomic historians, the period of the judges was an era of repeated faithlessness, an age in which Israel not only denied its covenant with Yahweh again and again, but an age in which Israel responded to each new act of divine compassion by renewed faithlessness.

The rule of the judges ends on a somber note. One characteristic of ancient Israelite literary composition was moving from one section into another by merging the two sections at the point where they joined. Thus Amos 1:2 repeats Joel 3:16, and Ezra 1:1-3 repeats 2 Chronicles 36:22-23. It is possible to argue that Saul was either the last of the Israelite judges or the first of the Israelite kings. He displays traits of each because he stands at the point where the nation changed from rule by judge to rule by king. When we look at the last of the judges—Samuel and his sons—and the first of the kings—Saul—we find that the institution of the charismatic leader had fallen on evil days.

Samuel's career ended in disaster. Israel was defeated in battle by the Philistines, and the ark of Yahweh was captured by the enemy (1 Sam. 4-5). Samuel appointed his sons to be his successors, and his choice was unwise.

(1) When Samuel became old, he made his sons judges over Israel. (2) The name of his first-born son was Joel, and the name of his second, Abijah; they were judges in Beersheba. (3) Yet his sons did not walk in his ways, but turned aside after gain; they took bribes and perverted justice. (1 Sam. 8:1-3.)

Saul's effectiveness is more difficult to evaluate. He had the misfortune to be followed by David. David not only founded a new dynasty—rooting out Saul's family to protect his own claim to the throne—but he so captured the hearts and minds of his people that the historians who wrote the story of his rise to the throne (1 Sam. 16:14–2 Sam. 5:12) tried by various means to blacken Saul's character and reputation. When we report traces of deterioration in Saul, therefore, we may actually be reporting only the campaign of vilification of Saul undertaken by David's court historians. Even so, the Deuteronomic historians accepted the Davidic dynastic history, using it to state their own understanding of the history of Israel.

Their understanding of the first part of Israelite history can be stated quite briefly. Charismatic leadership had failed. It could not achieve a lasting faithfulness in Israel, it could not be passed on from father to son to provide political stability, and it destroyed the men through whom it acted. We are told twice that Saul raved when aroused by the spirit-possession of prophets (1 Sam. 10:10; 19:18-24), and that the spirit-possession Saul himself displayed during the defense of Jabesh-Gilead (1 Sam. 11:5-11) became an evil spirit which destroyed his sanity (1 Sam. 16:14; 18:10).

The second period in the Deuteronomic History overlaps the first in the person of Saul. He was, as has already been said, both the last of the judges and the first of the kings. David, however, was the greatest of Israel's kings, and the only one to establish a long-lived dynasty. His grip on the memories of his nation was so firm that nine centuries later Jewish Christians claimed the authority of his name as part of their affirmations about Jesus of Nazareth (as in Matt. 1:1, 6, 17; Lk. 2:4).

His achievements were remarkable. He captured Jerusalem and made it his capital city (2 Sam. 5:6-9). He united the tribes of Israel and the Canaanites. He established an empire which ranged as far north as Damascus and as far south as the frontier of Egypt, from Philistia on the west to the plains across the Jordan on the east (2 Sam. 8:1-14). For the first time, the Israelites supported royal officials (2 Sam. 8:15-18; 20:23-26) and a band of mercenaries which served both as the royal bodyguard and as the core of an army made up largely of tribal militia (2 Sam. 23:8-39).

Great though David's political and military importance was, his cultic importance was greater. He gave the Israelites a new understanding of the relationship of God to nation, and he seems to have introduced into the worship of Israel rites taken from a Canaanite royal cult. We find only traces of this in the Deuteronomic History, however, and have to wait for our study of the Psalms for a fuller understanding of it.

The Deuteronomic historians assert four times that God had chosen David and his descendants to rule Israel forever.[6] This is reported first in the form of a prophetic legend. God, through Nathan the prophet, reproved David for his desire to build a temple, but the reproof became blessing when Nathan assured David that Yahweh

(11) . . . declares to you that the LORD will make you a house. (12) When your days are fulfilled and you lie down with your fathers, I will raise up your son after you, who shall come forth from your body, and I will establish his kingdom. . . . (16) And your house and your kingdom shall be made sure for ever before me; your throne shall be established for ever. (2 Sam. 7:11*b*, 12, 16.)

This is followed immediately by David's confirmation of the promise before God in prayer (2 Sam. 7:18-29). Late in David's reign, he faced a revolt led by his son Absalom, and a second rebellion led by Sheba son of Bichri, a Benjaminite. After the Deuteronomic historian reported David's suppression of both insurrections, he pictured David praising God's goodness and power in a hymn which closes:

> Great triumphs he gives to his king,
>   and shows steadfast love to his anointed,
>   to David, and his descendants for ever.
>   (2 Sam. 22:51.)

The fourth declaration of David's everlasting covenant with God now has the form of David's last will and testament (2 Sam. 23:1-7). Verse 5 is especially important.

> Yea, does not my house stand so with God?
>   For he has made with me an everlasting
>   covenant,
>   ordered in all things and secure.
> For will he not cause to prosper
>   all my help and my desire?

When we reconstruct the royal theology implied in the book of Psalms,[7] it becomes clear that the Deuteronomic historians were being highly selective in their report of the Davidic dynasty's understanding of the relationship of God, king, and nation. They were not quite as selective in their account of the changes David introduced into the rites of Israel's worship. He is pictured as bringing the various sacred symbols of the tribes into Jerusalem— a city which for centuries had been a center of Canaanite worship— using rites and symbols which shocked his strict Yahwist wife, Michal (2 Sam. 6). He also made his sons priests (2 Sam. 8:18), a practice which must have seemed reasonable to his Canaanite subjects who believed the king himself to be divine. All of this was religious syncretism, the attempt to blend together the worship of the gods of Canaan and the God of Israel.

The Deuteronomic historians were to hold such syncretism to be sin in all later kings. David, however, was not condemned for it. Part of the reason for the Deuteronomic approval of David probably was the interpretation put upon his success as a king. If we remember that the royal covenant, which provided the structure for the Israelite understanding of its relationship with Yahweh, ended with the promise of blessing if the covenant were kept or curse if it were violated, we can see how reasonable it would seem to conclude that tremendous blessing proves the presence of divine approval. David's great achievements must have been viewed as divine blessing. Whatever David did, therefore, the Deuteronomic historians had to conclude that he did it with God's approval. It also is true, however, that the picture of David that shines through the history is of a strangely attractive man, impulsive and tyrannical, yet humble before God. This quality may have been more important to the Deuteronomic historians than we realize. It may have made it possible for them to ignore his religious syncretism, for they did ignore it.

The second stage of the Deuteronomic History ends in the reign of Solomon (1 Kings 1–11). Solomon is so great a king in Israelite history that we allow the reports of the splendors of his reign to conceal from us what really is being said. He seized the throne illegally from an older brother and consolidated his hold on it by a blood purge. He fastened upon his people such an oppressive reign that the northern tribes tried to revolt during his lifetime and did break away after his death. The splendors of his court were paid for partly by slavery imposed upon all the nation. He enlarged the standing army but lost parts of the empire conquered by David because he used his army to garrison a restive nation.

That which is pictured for us by the Deuteronomic historians is the deterioration of the new relationship of God, king, and people begun by David. Solomon was a completely Canaanite king. Even the Temple he built for Yahweh was Canaanite in plan and decoration! [8] The religious syncretism begun under David reached its consummation in Solomon. Yahweh had become a baal, and the worship of Yahweh had become a Canaanite fertility cult. The king, who had been the adopted son of Yahweh anointed as messiah to rule over the people of Yahweh, now claimed the rights of divinity for himself and asserted ownership of the people he ruled.

The second part of the Deuteronomic History thus also ended in failure. Israel itself had been faithless during the period of the judges; but in one generation, the kings chosen by God to replace the judges also became faithless and led the people more deeply into apostasy. As Solomon's reign drew to a close, the shadows of impending judgment began to gather. The Edomites attempted revolt, the northern province of the empire broke away to form the kingdom of Aram—or Syria—and the northern tribes tried to revolt and failed. Their leader, however, escaped to lead a second rebellion after Solomon's death (1 Kings 11:14-40). The end of the united monarchy came in the hour of Solomon's death. The northern tribes rejected the rule of Rehoboam his son (1 Kings 12:1-17). [9]

The third stage of the Deuteronomic History reports the destruction of the monarchy. Two Israelite kingdoms, neither strong enough to survive, came out of the breakup of Solomon's kingdom. The northern, called Israel or Ephraim, included the ten northern tribes, the larger population, and the greater resources. It knew hours of greatness under the reigns of Omri, Ahab, and Jeroboam II, although we discover this either through Assyrian records or deduce it from cryptic statements in Kings. The Deuteronomic historians were concerned only with the faithfulness or faithlessness of the northern kings. All were judged to be faithless, and this formula was used:

In the _____ year of _____, king of Judah, _____, the son of _____ began to reign over Israel in _____, and he reigned _____ years. He did what was evil in the sight of the LORD, and followed the sins of Jeroboam the son of Nebat, which he made Israel to sin; he did not depart from them.

The sin of Jeroboam was twofold: he ordered Israel to worship golden calves as the god that had brought the nation out of Egypt (1 Kings 12:28; 2 Kings 10:29), and he commanded Israel to worship in Bethel and Dan, rather than in Jerusalem (1 Kings 12:27, 29-30). The Deuteronomic historians held this to be repudiation of the covenant with Yahweh. This, and adopting Canaanite ways of worship, eventually bore fruit in the destruction of Samaria and the northern kingdom (2 Kings 17:1-18).

The royal shrine for the house of David was Jerusalem, of course, and thus the Judaean monarchy escaped the second part of the accusation made against the kings of Israel. Nevertheless, the Deuteronomic report of the history of the southern kingdom differs from the account of the northern monarchy only in details. Individual southern kings were openly faithless to Yahweh, such as Ahaz who substituted the worship of Ashur, the god of Assyria, for the worship of Yahweh in the Temple in Jerusalem (2 Kings 16:5-16), and Manasseh who embraced many foreign cults (2 Kings 21:1-9). Other kings were given qualified approval, with their attempt to destroy Canaanite worship being recorded (of Asa: 1 Kings 15:11-15; and of Jehoshaphat: 1 Kings 22:43, 46). Such faithfulness, however, did not protect Jehoash (2 Kings 11:17–12:3, 17-20) or Amaziah (2 Kings 14:3-6, 11-14, 19-20) from catastrophe. Both were defeated in battle and killed by their subjects when they fled.

Not even the efforts of the two great reforming kings, Hezekiah and Josiah, could prevent catastrophe. Hezekiah repudiated Ahaz' worship of Ashur and revolted against the Assyrians, only to be crushed and forced to pay heavy tribute (2 Kings 18:1-8, 13-16). Josiah, whose reformation seems to have been based upon the Deuteronomic Code—something of which the Deuteronomic historians surely approved—did experience the blessing of independence for a time but met death in battle twelve years after his reformation (2 Kings 22:1–23:30).

There is some disorder in the Deuteronomic History at this point. An oracle by Hulda, a prophetess, was preserved which declared that Judah would be punished for its prolonged faithlessness in spite of the reformation but that Josiah would die in peace (2 Kings 22:15-20). He did not die in peace. Furthermore, Deuteronomic praise for Josiah is now linked directly to condemnation of the nation he ruled:

(25) Before him there was no king like him, who turned to the LORD with all his heart and with all his soul and with all his might, according to all the law of Moses; nor did any like him arise after him. (26) Still the LORD did not turn from the fierceness of his great wrath, by which his anger was kindled against Judah, because of all the provocations with which Manasseh had provoked him. (27) And the LORD said, "I will remove Judah also out of my sight, as I have removed Israel, and I will cast off this city which I have chosen, Jerusalem, and the house of which I said, My name shall be there." (2 Kings 23:25-27; see also 21:10-15.)

The end came swiftly. The last reforming king was killed in 609 B.C. Jerusalem was captured thirteen years later in 598. Twelve years later in 586, it was captured a second time and destroyed. The monarchy had been no more successful in guiding the people of God faithfully before him than the judges had been. A theme in the Deuteronomic report of the founding of the monarchy may come from this time. We are told that the Israelites asked Samuel to select a king for them after Samuel's sons proved to be corrupt judges. When Samuel consulted God in the matter,

(7) ... the LORD said to Samuel, "Hearken to the voice of the people in all that they say to you; for they have not rejected you, but they have rejected me from being king over them. (8) According to all the deeds which they have done to me, from the day I brought them up out of Egypt even to this day, forsaking me and serving other gods, so they are also doing to you. (9) Now then, hearken to their voice; only, you shall solemnly warn them, and show them the ways of the king who shall reign over them." (1 Sam. 8:7-9.)

But the people refused to hear Samuel's warning (vss. 11-20). Thus the Deuteronomic historians came eventually to believe that both the deeds of individual kings and the desire of the people to be ruled by kings were faithlessness.

3

The Deuteronomic History has been studied from three different viewpoints: for the sake of its contributions to the reconstruction of the history of ancient Israel, for the sake of its contributions to the history of the religion of ancient Israel, and because of its own theological affirmations. Each of these viewpoints asks its own kinds of questions, and each comes to an understanding of these biblical books appropriate to its own interests.

A. *The task of the historian is to identify each source used by the Deuteronomic historians,* to evaluate the degree of reliability of each source, and to add to those sources he has found and tested other sources for the study of this period made available to him by archaeologists in order to create a history of ancient Israel from the period of the judges to the end of the monarchy. His interest in the Deuteronomic History leads him, therefore, to a series of conclusions about its historicity.[10]

He will note the many cases in which the Deuteronomic historians failed to report from their sources information which we today view as important—such as Ahab's participation in a coalition which stopped an Assyrian invasion in 853 B.C.—or the instances in which the Deuteronomic historians mix nonhistorical legend and historically reliable legend with a free hand—as in the various stories told about the rise of Saul to the throne. The end result can be a negative impression of the Deuteronomic History if we fail to see the significance of that which has been found.

One result of the historian's source analysis is the discovery that the Deuteronomic historians were quite careful in their reporting of the sources they used. Their history gives us an impression of roughness, even of confusion, which can now be understood. Their respect for the traditions of their people was so great that they preserved accurately those traditions even when they reflected views at odds with their own.

The second result of the historian's study of the Deuteronomic historians' use of their sources is a clearer understanding of the school's viewpoint. One way to discover the message these historians were trying to convey is by studying their editorial comments, the editorial framework they provided for the sources they quoted. Another way is to ponder the significance of the importance to them of the sources they used and the unimportance to them of the sources they ignored. By using both approaches to the study of the meaning of the Deuteronomic History, we reach a clearer, more trustworthy view of their message.

B. *The Deuteronomic History can also be studied for the sake of its contribution to the history of Israelite religion.* There often is a difference between the most elevated statements and practices of a faith and the beliefs and practices of those who are not leaders. The attempt to make this distinction, to describe the faith both of the average Israelite and of his spiritual leaders, and to trace the history of both levels of religion, is called the history of Israelite religion.

The Deuteronomic History is quite useful in this study. The mere fact that we can distinguish so often between the work of the Deuteronomic historians and the sources they used on the basis of differences in viewpoint is proof that the Deuteronomic religious beliefs were not the beliefs of all Israelites.

The Deuteronomists rejected human sacrifice but reported its presence without comment (1 Kings 16:34); they attacked fertility cult rites vigorously but reported David's fertility dance before the ark (2 Sam. 6:16-22); they opposed worship on the high places strongly, yet tell us that David averted God's anger by praying to him from the high place on which the Canaanite Arauna had a threshing floor (2 Sam. 24:18-25). The Deuteronomic historians' description of the cleansing of the worship of Judah by Josiah includes a detailed and an incredible list of pagan gods and alien rites (2 Kings 23:4-14). [11]

The care with which the Deuteronomic historians reported beliefs and rites of which they strongly disapproved is an important clue in seeking the meaning of the history. All recent studies of the work of the Deuteronomic School confirm the judgment of an earlier generation of scholars: it reflects the same intense and pure Yahwism found in the great prophets. It also should be said that the accusations of false worship directed by the school against their contemporaries is echoed—in general and in all details—by those same prophets.

That which begins to emerge in the use of the Deuteronomic History as a source for writing the history of Israelite religion is the presence in ancient Israel of a bitter and persistent clash between two religious traditions. We call one Israelite Yahwism, and the other Canaanite Baalism.

One tradition, which was described in the previous chapter, sought to worship Yahweh, the God who had made himself known to Israel in a series of saving events centered in the Exodus from Egypt. This sacred tradition laid upon Israel obedience to a divine law which preserved and strengthened the people of God. The other tradition came into the life of Israel through its association with the Canaanites in the affairs of the nation of which both peoples were a part. Its followers worshiped Baal as the divine procreator, with rites designed to guarantee the perpetuation of life, and venerated the king as Baal's earthly representative. This religion was so severely attacked in every detail by the prophets that it will be described more fully in the next two chapters.

C. *The third viewpoint by which the Deuteronomic History can be studied is the theological.* Here we want to know what the Deuteronomic historians believed about the relationship between God and Israel. This is a proper inquiry because the ancient Israelites often turned to narration when they wished to present, or to debate, theological issues;[12] and we have already discovered that the other kinds of approach to this history eventually lead us to theological judgments.

The Deuteronomic historians shared with the rest of the Deuteronomic School the belief that the covenant between a king and his subjects was like the covenant between God and his people. God is to be identified by name; the deeds which reveal his royal power are to be described by the community; the community is then to accept this God as its God and is to promise to be faithful; the royal will which the community is to obey is then stated; and the results of faithfulness or faithlessness to the covenant are defined. Descriptions of Yahweh's mighty, saving acts—the deeds upon which his right to be worshiped by Israel rests—are scattered throughout both the Deuteronomic Code and the Deuteronomic History. The Deuteronomic Code is the statement of the royal will of Yahweh. The blessings that were to follow obedience, and the curses that were to follow disobedience, are listed in the Deuteronomic Code (Deut. 27–28), and the Deuteronomic History is the description of the working out of such blessings or curses in the history of Israel.

One motif in the theology of the Deuteronomic History should not be overlooked, however. The repeated faithlessness of Israel under the judges finally brought an end to the history of the tribal confederation, but the faithlessness of Israel did not bring about an end to Israel. The sovereignty of God is pictured as displaying itself in the creation of the Davidic monarchy in a new outburst of blessing. Once again, however, the kings and the people proved faithless, and God acted once again in judgment. The Deuteronomic historians wrote in the ashes of the destruction of the monarchy and knew at first hand the bitterness of the woe God had brought upon them.

Nevertheless, it was out of this period that a prayer was placed in the record of the dedication of Solomon's Temple. Part of that prayer clearly reflects the life of Israel in the exile, and it therefore is the voice of the Deuteronomic historians speaking out of the exile.

(46) If they sin against thee—for there is no man who does not sin—and thou art angry with them, and dost give them to an enemy, so that they are carried away captive to the land of the enemy, far off or near; (47) yet if they lay it to heart in the land to which they have been carried captive, and repent, and make supplication to thee in the land of their captors, saying, "We have sinned, and have acted perversely and wickedly"; (48) if they repent with all their mind and with all their heart in the land of their enemies, who carried them captive, and pray to thee toward their land, which thou gavest to their fathers, the city which thou hast chosen, and the house which I have built for thy name; (49) then hear thou in heaven thy dwelling place their prayer and their supplication, and maintain their cause (50) and forgive thy people who have sinned against thee, and all their transgressions which they have committed against thee; and grant them compassion in the sight of those who carried them captive, that they may have compassion on them. (1 Kings 8:46-50.)

Solomon's prayer during the dedication of his Temple came from the authors of the historical notation with which the history ends.

(27) And in the thirty-seventh year of the exile of Jehoiachin king of Judah, in the twelfth month, on the twenty-seventh day of the month, Evil-merodach king of Babylon, in the year that he began to reign, graciously freed Jehoiachin king of Judah from prison; (28) and he spoke kindly to him, and gave him a seat above the seats of the kings who were with him in Babylon. (29) So Jehoiachin put off his prison garments. And every day of his life he dined regularly at the king's table; (30) and for his allowance, a regular allowance was given him by the king, every day a portion, as long as he lived. (2 Kings 25:27-30.)

This is not an impressive event in the annals of empires, but the Deuteronomic historians saw in it the promise of something far more important to them than the rise and fall of great empires. The same God whose just anger had destroyed the Israelite monarchy had again heard the prayers of his people and would again pour out upon them the blessing of his compassion. They did not know the form God's new saving acts would take. It was enough for them to be able to hope for that salvation. They had discovered anew, through the study of the history of their people, that their God was a great God who ruled them in justice and love.

NOTES

1. The remaining five historical books are Joshua, Ezra, Nehemiah, and 1 and 2 Chronicles. Chronicles is a *midrash* (the Jewish term for a commentary) on the Deuteronomic History, is very late, and displays a strong priestly interest. Ezra and Nehemiah, which describe the return from the Exile, are also late and show many similarities in style and viewpoint with the Priestly Source. Joshua contains three elements: a story of the invasion which blends into a single account once independent tribal histories, a description of the division of Canaan among the tribes written in a style similar to the style of the Priestly Source, and the early account of the Shechemite covenant renewal festival (Josh. 24).

2. The claim that there is a Deuteronomic Work rests both upon shared style and a unity of purpose and theme. For a judgment on the presence of shared style by a literary critic of a former generation—who did not claim that there was a Deuteronomic Work—see S. R. Driver, *A Criti-*

cal and Exegetical Commentary on Deuteronomy (New York: Charles
Scribner's Sons, 1903), pp. lxxvii-lxxxiii where seventy words and
phrases (listed in English translation) distinctive to the style of the
Deuteronomic School are given. Appearances of each outside the book
of Deuteronomy are also given, and the reader can determine for himself the number of these words and phrases which appear also in the
editorial framework of the historical books. The first defense of the
existence of the Deuteronomic Work was given by Martin Noth in his
*Überlieferungsgeschichtliche Studien, die sammelnden und bear-
beitenden Geschichtswerke im Alten Testament* (Tübingen: Max
Niemeyer, 1957), pp. 1-110. O. Eissfeldt, *The Old Testament, an
Introduction,* pp. 242-48, reviews this viewpoint, as well as another
possibility.
3. Accounting records for Nebuchadnezzar, the Babylonian king who imprisoned Jehoiachin, have been recovered which list the provisions set
aside for Jehoiachin's support. See Oppenheim, "Assyrian and Babylonian Historical Texts," in Pritchard, ed., *Ancient Near Eastern Texts,*
p. 308, and *The Ancient Near East, an Anthology,* p. 205.
4. James A. Montgomery, *A Critical and Exegetical Commentary on the
Books of Kings* (New York: Charles Scribner's Sons, 1951), pp. 30-41.
See also John Gray, *I and II Kings, a Commentary* (Philadelphia: The
Westminster Press, 1963), pp. 20-38.
5. For discussions of the meaning of "spirit" in the Old Testament, see
S. V. McCasland, "Spirit," *Interpreter's Dictionary of the Bible,* ed.
G. A. Buttrick, *et al.* (Nashville: Abingdon Press, 1962), Millar
Burrows, *An Outline of Biblical Theology* (Philadelphia: The West-
minster Press, 1946), pp. 74-76; Edmond Jacob, *Theology of the Old
Testament,* A. W. Heathcote and P. J. Allcock, trs. (New York: Harper
& Row, 1958), pp. 121-27.
6. The Hebrew term translated as "everlasting" seems to have designated
time extending indefinitely into past and future, not time without end.
See H. W. Robinson, *Inspiration and Revelation in the Old Testament*
(Oxford: The Clarendon Press, 1946), pp. 116-20.
7. For descriptions of the ideology of the kingship, see C. J. Gadd, *Ideas
of Divine Rule in the Ancient Near East* (London: Oxford University
Press, 1948 [H. Milford for The British Academy]); Henri Frankfort,
Kingship and the Gods (Chicago: University of Chicago Press, 1948),
Ivan Engnell, *Studies in Divine Kingship in the Ancient Near East*
(Uppsala: Almqvist & Wiksells, 1943); A. R. Johnson, *Sacral Kingship in Ancient Israel* (Cardiff: University of Wales Press, 1955);
K. R. Crim, *The Royal Psalms* (Richmond: John Knox Press, 1962).
8. G. E. Wright, *Biblical Archaeology,* pp. 136-45.
9. There is some reason to deduce Egyptian interference in the revolt
on the side of the northern tribes. Solomon had garrisoned the land with
chariots, the ancient equivalent to panzer units, and lightly armed

tribal levies would have been useless against them. Rehoboam inherited his father's army and could have been defeated only by a superior force, such as Egypt could deploy. The Egyptians list places captured which were in the north, even though Jerusalem had to pay tribute, and this suggests that the Egyptian Palestinian campaign mentioned in 1 Kings 14:25-26 may have included the reduction of Rehoboam's strongholds throughout the north. Finally, it should be remembered that unsuccessful rebels against Solomon fled to Egypt for sanctuary, thus implicating Egypt in their revolts. Both Noth, *The History of Israel*, p. 238, and Bright, *History of Israel*, pp. 231-32, reject this interpretation.

10. H. P. Smith, *A Critical and Exegetical Commentary on the Books of Samuel* (New York: Charles Scribner's Sons, 1899), and J. A. Montgomery, *A Critical and Exegetical Commentary on the Books of Kings*, relied primarily on literary criticism to identify the various sources used. H. W. Hertzberg, *I and II Samuel, a Commentary*, J. S. Bowden, tr. (Philadelphia: The Westminster Press, 1964), and Gray, *I and II Kings*, add form criticism to literary criticism. A similar evaluation can be made of the histories of Israel available. Robinson and Oesterley, in *A History of Israel*, rely primarily upon literary criticism for identifying the sources used, although both scholars were competent form critics. Noth, *The History of Israel*, uses both literary and form criticism. Bright, *History of Israel*, relies more heavily on extrabiblical sources to establish the reliability of the biblical materials.

11. For histories of Israelite religion using data preserved in the Deuteronomic History, see James Muilenburg, "The History of the Religion of Israel," *The Interpreter's Bible*, I, 292-348, esp. pp. 305-17; Elmer A. Leslie, *Old Testament Religion in the Light of its Canaanite Background* (Nashville: Cokesbury Press, 1936), pp. 95-162; Oesterley and Robinson, *Hebrew Religion: Its Origin and Development* (New York: The Macmillan Company, 1930), pp. 168-92; Pfeiffer, *Religion in the Old Testament: The History of a Spiritual Triumph*, pp. 58-116.

12. See G. von Rad, *Old Testament Theology*, I, 115-21.

IV

THE PRE-EXILIC PROPHETS

Thus far we have examined the salvation history recorded in the Hexateuch and the explanation of God's punishment of Israel given by the Deuteronomic historians. We turn now to the work of the prophets.

Fourteen books of the Old Testament use the names of prophets in their titles.[1] Five of these preserve words of the great prophets. These are the books of Amos, Hosea, Isaiah, Jeremiah, and Ezekiel. The book of Isaiah records the work of a school founded by the prophet Isaiah, and both the founder of the school and one of his disciples belong in any list of the great prophets. We do not know the name of the great disciple and simply call him the Second Isaiah. Thus the six prophets in chronological order are Amos, Hosea, Isaiah, Jeremiah, Ezekiel, and the Second Isaiah.

Five of these men lived between the writing of the Yahwist strand in the Hexateuch—the first complete account of the salvation history as we know it today—and the Deuteronomic History. A part of the importance of these prophets is that they made the writing of the Deuteronomic History possible. It is always easy to believe that God is at work when things go well. Seeing his presence in disaster is more difficult—and more important. The Deuteronomic historians learned this from the first five of Israel's great prophets. But if we turn to the study of the prophets expecting immediately to see for ourselves their greatness, we will be disappointed. What a queer jumble of nonsense these books seem to be!

If what we are told about the prophets is true, they acted strangely. Hosea married "a wife of harlotry" (Hos. 1:2-3); Isaiah tramped the streets of Jerusalem naked for three years (Is. 20:1-3); Jeremiah was in so much trouble that first the priests (Jer. 26:7-19) and then the princes (Jer. 37:11-15) had him arrested. Ezekiel tied himself up and lay on one side for three hundred and ninety days, then rolled over and lay on the other side for forty days (Ezek. 4:4-8). One wonders if respectable people wanted to be seen in the company of these men.

Their words also seem odd at times. When a priest in the royal chapel in Bethel accused Amos of treason, Amos seems not only to have admitted it but to have turned on the priest with a curse (Amos 7:10-17). Hosea described Gilead, where the monarchy began, as "a city of evil doers, tracked with blood," and said that the priests acted like robbers who "murder on the way to Shechem" (Hos. 6:8-9). Isaiah delivered a "sermon" which was little more than a list of villages on the Assyrian invasion route (Is. 10:27*b*-32). Jeremiah once described his opponents as those who "commit adultery and walk in lies" (Jer. 23:14).

Strange, uncomfortable men! Few of us would welcome them as friends or would want one as a pastor. Few of us, after our first attempt to read them, find them agreeable or even intelligible. Even in our bewilderment, however, we have to admit that they spoke with power, clarity, and beauty. Amos ended a description of God's anger:

> But let justice roll down like waters,
>   and righteousness like an ever-flowing
>   stream.
>
> (Amos 5:24.)

The message of divine compassion that finally came to Hosea awes us with its profundity and simplicity. He heard God declare:

> I will not execute my fierce anger,
>   I will not again destroy Ephraim;
> for I am God and not man,
>   the Holy One in your midst,
>   and I will not come to destroy.
>
> (Hos. 11:9.)

These prophets reached such heights that their words can still stand as some of the most profound in our heritage. If you find this difficult to believe, read Isaiah 9:2-7 or 52:13–53:12. Strange and obscure though the prophets may be, they are so important that we need to know something about each one.

In order to make this possible, we will discuss each of the six in order.[2] General questions, such as what a prophet thought about his calling, how his contemporaries viewed him, and the uniqueness of the prophetic message, will be examined at the end. The prophets believed themselves to be God's spokesmen. The first person singular pronoun in their oracles usually refers back to God, not to the prophet. A chronological chart follows chapter 5. It will help you to place these men in the history of their age.

AMOS

Amos tells us that he had been a herdsman, a layman rather than a clergyman, who lived near Tekoa in the southern kingdom.[3] He had been commanded by God to prophesy against the northern kingdom during the reign of Jeroboam II (786-746 B.C. Amos 7:14-15; 1:1). Other than this we really know nothing about him, and silence about the prophet's life holds true for most of the prophetic books. The silence was so complete for the Second Isaiah that we lack even his name. We can date the ministries of all the prophets however, and this is important because they believed that God was disclosing himself in the events of their day.

Jeroboam II was a relatively powerful king. Israel's frontiers were expanded during his reign, and historians for the northern kingdom felt that this proved that Yahweh was pleased with both king and people (2 Kings 14:25). Amos disagreed.

The prophet reacted satirically to the piety of the Israelites. He urged them to avoid all their shrines if they sought Yahweh and to visit the great shrines at Bethel and Gilgal in order to sin.

> 4) "Come to Bethel, and transgress;
>   to Gilgal, and multiply transgression;
>   bring your sacrifices every morning,
>   your tithes every three days;

5) offer a sacrifice of thanksgiving of
   that which is leavened,
   and proclaim freewill offerings, publish them;
   for so you love to do, O people of Israel!"
                                        says the Lord God.
                                           (Amos 4:4-5.)

Injustice went hand in hand with false worship (Amos 2:6-8),
and the powerful exploited the weak (Amos 4:1-3; 5:10-12; 6:4-7).
No worship could be so splendid that it could replace doing the
right.

21) I hate, I despise your feasts,
    and I take no delight in your solemn assemblies.
22) Even though you offer me your burnt offerings and
    cereal offerings,
    I will not accept them,
    and the peace offerings of your fatted beasts
    I will not look upon.
23) Take away from me the noise of your songs;
    to the melody of your harps I will not listen.
24) But let justice roll down like waters,
    and righteousness like an ever-flowing stream.
                                           (Amos 5:21-24.)

In all this, Amos seems to have been looking back at the
ancient covenant festival celebrated at Shechem before the
founding of the monarchy. We have already examined the ancient
salvation history which was retold during the festival, and we can
find traces of it in Amos. Israel had been brought out of Egypt by
Yahweh (Amos 9:7) and had been led through the wilderness for
forty years (Amos 2:10; 5:25). We believe that the Shechem
festival also contained commandments and curses, rules governing
Israel's life under Yahweh and penalties for disobedience. If
Deuteronomy 27:15-26 is a list of curses like those used in the
festival, Amos recalled the rite more often than we might at first
suspect. Deuteronomy 27:15 is echoed in Amos 5:26; 8:14. The

kind of sexual conduct permitted in Canaanite religion but condemned in Deuteronomy 27:20-23 is repudiated in Amos 2:7
also. Those who warp the judicial process for personal benefit are
condemned both in Deuteronomy 27:25 and in Amos 5:10, 12,
15.

Thus Amos was a conservative. He looked back to a time when
Israel worshiped Yahweh differently than it did in his day. But
he added something to the tradition also.

The heart of the matter for Amos was the royal freedom and
power of Yahweh. As we have just seen, there is good reason to
believe that the prophet accepted the Shechemite tradition. This
tradition claimed that Israel came into existence as a people because
Yahweh decided to rescue it from destruction in Egypt and to
make it his own. He did rescue the clans and tribes from disaster,
offered them the terms of his agreement, and promised them
further help if they would accept his rule. Amos 3:1, which
mentions the exodus, implies a demand for obedience: "Hear this
word that the LORD has spoken against you, O people of Israel,
against the whole family which I brought up out of the land of
Egypt." Verse 2 describes what would happen if Israel, asked to
live under an agreement with Yahweh, insisted instead on living
as if it had an agreement with a different god.

> You only have I known
>   of all the families of the earth;
> therefore I will punish you
>   for all your iniquities.

The religion of the peoples among whom the Israelites lived
after they invaded Palestine was a form of nature worship. The
gods, whose blessings were believed to be the abundance flowing
from the fertility of flocks, herds, fields, and vineyards, were held
to be active in the changes of the seasons. The coming of the
rains which made crops possible was a revival of the power of
Baal, the god of rain and fertility. The dry heat of summer which

ripened—or killed—the grain was the reign of the god of death. The god of death obviously could reign only when the god of life did not rule. Thus the seasons were thought to mirror the changing fortunes of the gods as they fought among themselves for the control of the world.[4]

Man's worship was designed to encourage and to strengthen the deities in their struggles. We find it nearly impossible to believe that some forms of the worship described were really followed, yet Amos (Amos 2:7-8), Hosea (Hos. 4:11-14) and Jeremiah (Jer. 2:20-25) all insisted that they were. From these passages we can identify cultic promiscuity and ritual drunkenness as two of these cult practices. These were believed to be necessary because they were thought to encourage the divine procreator.

If we are right in seeing in the curses in Deuteronomy 27 an echo of the ancient Shechemite Yahweh cult, we see this religion picturing God as blessing men by giving them a healthy, orderly society. His will was to be seen in the rules preserving such a society. The family is to be strong (Deut. 27:16); men are to respect property rights (Deut. 27:17), the unfortunate have the right to the help of others (Deut. 27:18-19), and the judicial system is to be maintained by truthfulness, not by force (Deut. 27:24).

Could men worship both Baal and Yahweh? Could they worship Baal by calling him Yahweh? Could they worship Yahweh as if he were Baal? These two gods demanded different kinds of obedience and were believed to give different kinds of blessing. Could the two religions blend? Amos knew that they could not, and he condemned as evil piety which used Yahweh's name in the worship of Baal.

> 6) Thus says the LORD:
> "For three transgressions of Israel,
>   and for four, I will not revoke the
>   punishment;
> because they sell the righteous for silver,
>   and the needy for a pair of shoes—

7) they that trample the head of the poor into
    the dust of the earth,
    and turn aside the way of the afflicted;
    a man and his father go in to the same maiden,
    so that my holy name is profaned;
8) they lay themselves down beside every altar
    upon garments taken in pledge;
    and in the house of their God they drink
    the wine of those who have been fined."

                        (Amos 2:6-8.)

Amos was not the first to see that Yahwism and Baalism could not mix. Elijah realized it earlier. The story of fire falling from heaven (1 Kings 18) is a popular memory of his message, just as the record of his bitter dispute with Ahab over a judicial murder (1 Kings 21) is another memory of the same message. Many of the prophets shared this insight both before and after Amos.

The reason which Amos gave for the incompatibility of Yahwism and Baalism is that which marks him as unique. Yahweh was the divine king, and kings will not rule subjects who try to serve other kings at the same time. If Israel tried to serve Yahweh and Baal, Yahweh would punish rather than rule.

13) "Behold, I will press you down in your place,
    as a cart full of sheaves presses down.
14) Flight shall perish from the swift,
    and the strong shall not retain his strength,
    nor shall the mighty save his life;
15) he who handles the bow shall not stand,
    and he who is swift of foot shall not save himself,
    nor shall he who rides the horse save his life;
16) and he who is stout of heart among the mighty
    shall flee away naked in that day,"

                    says the LORD.

                        (Amos 2:13-16.)

97

One of the Canaanite myths being used by some Israelites to describe Yahweh told how the savior god had to struggle constantly to maintain himself against another deity who wanted the world to revert to chaos. The battle raged year after year, producing the changes of the seasons. One day—so ran the myth—the savior god would defeat the chaos god completely. Then everything that the chaos deity brought to pass would cease. New life, health, wealth, children, and peace were gifts from the savior god and would flow endlessly. As the unknown author of an addition to the book of Amos put it,

> "Behold, the days are coming," says the Lord,
>   "when the plowman shall overtake the reaper
>   and the treader of grapes him who sows the seed;
> the mountains shall drip sweet wine,
>   and all the hills shall flow with it."
> (Amos 9:13.)

When the Israelites used this myth to describe Yahweh's activity, they identified Yahweh as the savior god of the myth. He had become Baal. Yahweh-as-Baal was engaged each year in a battle with the god of chaos. At some time in the future Yahweh-as-Baal would have his day. But Amos said of that day:

> 18) Woe to you who desire the day of the Lord!
>   Why would you have the day of the Lord?
>   It is darkness, and not light;
> 19) as if a man fled from a lion,
>   and a bear met him;
>   or went into the house and leaned with his hand
>   against the wall,
>   and a serpent bit him.
> 20) Is not the day of the Lord darkness, and not light,
>   and gloom with no brightness in it?
> (Amos 5:18-20.)

Yahweh would have a day, but it would be a day of agony and death.

Yahweh was not locked in a struggle with a chaos god. He had won that battle long ago. He was engaged in a struggle with Israel's faithlessness. He was not a cosmic assembly line turning out blessings except when interrupted by another god. He was in complete command. He was as much the source of evil as of good (Amos 4:6-11). His day would be a time when he punished a rebellious people. Had Israel served him as he had commanded, it would have been a day of blessing. Since Israel had betrayed its promise to obey, it would be a day of pain.

Thus, while it is true to say that Amos did look back to the Shechemite covenant as the right form of the worship of Yahweh— and to this extent was a conservative—it also is true that he saw clearly that Yahweh was King and was as free to bless or to punish as was any earthly king. If he were to be expected to bless as reward for obedience, he also could be expected to punish for disobedience. If the part played in the creation myth by Yahweh-as-Baal made it hard to believe that Yahweh could punish, the myth was wrong. Yahweh was not a baal.

HOSEA

The unimportance of knowing many of the details of the life of a prophet is well shown by the book of Hosea.[5] There was a prophet named Hosea son of Beeri, and we are told the story of his marriage, (Hos. 1–3 in part). But it is very difficult to expand our knowledge of the prophet's personal life beyond this.

Some have said that Gomer, the prophet's wife, was a cult prostitute because she is called a wife of harlotry, but the more accurate translation, "wife of harlotries" suggests that she shared in the worship of Baal which the prophet elsewhere called "playing the harlot" (Hos. 4:10). Others have claimed that the prophet was a farmer because he mentioned agricultural products (Hos. 2:8-9) or a baker because he had seen an oven in use (Hos. 7:4).

99

But one might as well believe him to have been a vintner (Hos. 4:11) or a shepherd (Hos. 5:6). The simplest explanation for these passages is that Hosea, like the other great prophets, was an accurate observer of daily life. These are not hints of his occupation.

Nor do we really know when his ministry ended. Hosea 1:4-5. makes it clear that he started to prophesy before the end of the reign of the dynasty of Jehu. The last of this dynasty was Zechariah, the son of Jeroboam II, who was killed in a revolution six months after he came to the throne (2 Kings 15:10). Since the year was 746 B.C., we know that Hosea was at work before that date. But the end of his ministry? In 734 B.C., the Israelites and the Syrians invaded Judah in what is called the Syro-Ephraimitic War, but Assyria attacked the invaders from the rear and defeated them. Scholars have debated vigorously whether or not there are traces of the terrible defeat Israel suffered at the hands of Assyria in the oracles of Hosea. The mere fact that they have had to debate the question proves that the situation is not clear. All we really know about Hosea's dates is that he was working at the time of the end of the rule of the dynasty of Jehu. He did not witness the destruction of Samaria in 721 B.C.

In many ways, his message is like that of Amos. He mentioned various parts of the canonical saving history: the exodus from Egypt (Hos. 2:15?; 11:1; 13:4), the wilderness wandering (Hos. 12:9; 13:5); and he described Shechem as a shrine (Hos. 6:9). He referred again and again to Egypt as a place of bondage, either in the past or possibly again in the future (Hos. 7:16; 8:13; 9:3; 11:5). He also condemned many of the acts disapproved of in the curses in Deuteronomy 27, as did Amos. Hosea 4:17; 8:5; 10:5-6; 11:2; 13:2; 14:8 parallel Deuteronomy 27:15. Hosea is the only one of the six great prophets to mention the prohibition (Deut. 27:17) against moving landmarks (Hos. 5:10). The prophet shared the condemnation of Canaanite ritual sexual practices mentioned in Deuteronomy 27:20-23 (Hos. 4:10, 13-16), the prohibition of murder in secret (Deut. 27:24; Hos.

6:9), and the curse on those who refuse to obey the commandments included in the covenant with Yahweh (Deut. 27:26; Hos. 4:6; 6:7; 8:1, 12). As in the case of Amos, we can say confidently that Hosea knew and accepted the most ancient Yahwist traditions of his people.

He also agreed with Amos that Yahweh was as free to destroy as to bless. This is so strong a theme in Hosea that several readings of the book leave the feeling that the prophet talked about little else. The names he gave his children were key words in the message of judgment, and the third child, *Lo-ami*, "not my people," ran about the village with a name proclaiming to everyone that his father believed that the covenant had ended (Hos. 1:4-9). Everyone reading this prophet discovers sooner or later the lines which seem most terrible to him. I would suggest Hosea 9:10-14.

> 10) Like grapes in the wilderness,
>   I found Israel.
>   Like the first fruit on the fig tree,
>   in its first season,
>   I saw your fathers.
>   But they came to Baal-peor,
>   and consecrated themselves to Baal,
>   and became detestable like the thing they
>   loved.
> 11) Ephraim's glory shall fly away like a bird—
>   no birth, no pregnancy, no conception!
> 12) Even if they bring up children,
>   I will bereave them till none is left.
>   Woe to them
>   when I depart from them!
> 13) Ephraim's sons, as I have seen, are destined
>   for a prey;
>   Ephraim must lead forth his sons to slaughter.
> 14) Give them, O LORD—
>   what wilt thou give?
>   Give them a miscarrying womb
>   and dry breasts.

I Will Be Your God

Amos declared that the future of Israel would be destruction. It had defied the power of the God who had made himself known in a salvation history, and God's love had become wrath. Amos stated this by rejecting the role given Yahweh in the creation myth in popular Israelite religion. Yahweh's day of triumph would not be victory over the chaos god. That had been won ages ago. His day of triumph would be the time when he punished Israel for its faithlessness. Hosea also rejected the popular use of the creation myth. First he quoted a hymn based upon it.

> 1) Come, let us return to the LORD;
>   for he has torn, that he may heal us;
>   he has stricken, and he will bind us up.
> 2) After two days he will revive us;
>   on the third day he will raise us up,
>   that we may live before him.
> 3) Let us know, let us press on to know the LORD;
>   his going forth is sure as the dawn;
>   he will come to us as the showers,
>   as the spring rains that water the earth.
>   (Hos. 6:1-3.)

Yahweh's power to bless was pictured in the myth reflected in this hymn as increasing or decreasing as the power of the chaos god decreased or increased, a fluctuation of power reflected in the cycle of the seasons. The misfortunes of Yahweh's people were dismissed as being inevitable in the nature of things. Misfortune would always be followed by renewed blessing when Yahweh's power increased again. But Hosea, speaking for Yahweh, cried:

> 4) What shall I do with you, O Ephraim?
>   What shall I do with you, O Israel? [6]
>   Your love is like a morning cloud,
>   like the dew that goes early away.
> 5) Therefore I have hewn them by the prophets,
>   I have slain them by the words of my mouth,
>   and my judgment goes forth as the light.

6) For I desire steadfast love and not sacrifice,
   the knowledge of God, rather than burnt
   offerings.

(Hos. 6:4-6.)

The basis of Yahweh's relationship to his people was obedience to his will, not his struggles with another god. No other god was involved in Israel's affairs.

The uniqueness of Hosea is expressed in three passages, of which Hosea 11:9 is typical:

I will not execute my fierce anger,
   I will not again destroy Ephraim;
for I am God and not man,
   the Holy One in your midst,
   and I will not come to destroy.
(See also 14:1-4.)

This is the first appearance in the Hebrew-Christian tradition of the loving forgiveness of God, and it seems to have emerged out of the agony of the prophet's marriage.

Chapters 1 through 3 of the book of Hosea reflect a tragedy in the prophet's life. The language is so confused, and there have been so many later additions, that several reconstructions of the situation have been made. One is as follows:

Hosea married Gomer—Hosea 1:2 is a later interpretation of the event—and had three children, each given a name reflecting his message (Hos. 1:3-9; vs. 7 is later). By the birth of the third child, *Lo-ami*, Hosea had discovered that Gomer was participating in the kind of worship which he held to be rebellion against Yahweh. Since that cult required promiscuity, it not only was disloyal to Yahweh, it raised questions about the identity of the child's father. Thus Hosea experienced a double betrayal: Gomer had betrayed marriage vows he held to be sacred, and she had betrayed the God for whom Hosea was a spokesman. Her conduct, regardless of the motives that may have led her into it, announced to the community her contempt for Hosea's calling. He equated his marital tragedy with the tragedy of the relationship between Yahweh and Israel, and his statement of his divorce from Gomer becomes a description of Yahweh's repudiation of Israel (Hos. 2:2-13).

Chapter 3 speaks of an unnamed woman whom Hosea loves. Since the parallel between Hosea's life and Yahweh's relationship with Israel is maintained (Hos. 3:3-4), it seems likely that the woman is still Gomer. She is now pictured some time after the divorce. Hosea still loves her in spite of her offense, so much that he must punish her in the desperate hope of making her see her sin, repudiate it, and return to him. Once again the prophet saw the parallel between his agony and Yahweh's. Yahweh also would punish Israel in order to cleanse it of its faithlessness (Hos. 2:14). Then a new and lasting covenant could be made. "And I will betroth you to me for ever; I will betroth you to me in righteousness and in justice, in steadfast love, and in mercy. I will betroth you to me in faithfulness; and you shall know the LORD." (Hos. 2:19-20.)

It is most disturbing that biblical proclamations of the love of God rise out of the depths of man's suffering. Is it possible that we speak too glibly and cheaply of God's love?

ISAIAH OF JERUSALEM

The book of Isaiah contains sixty-six chapters. Many Christians have felt that to deny authorship of any of these to Isaiah is to deny his greatness. This would be true if quantity meant quality, but a large number of disciples working over several centuries is also proof of Isaiah's greatness. Those who claim that Isaiah himself produced only about fifteen of the sixty-six chapters do not believe that the rest of the book is a rubbish heap onto which stray bits of odds and ends were dumped. Most of the rest of the book contains the words of Isaiah's followers.[7]

Remarks in verses assigned to Isaiah make it clear that he

prophesied for at least four decades, perhaps longer. He became a prophet "in the year that King Uzziah died" (Is. 6:1), 742 B.C., and he described precisely the situation in Judah after the Assyrian invasion of 701 (Is. 1:7-9). He witnessed some vast and disturbing events.

Two years after he became a prophet, Tiglath-pileser III came to the throne of Assyria. By 738 B.C. the Assyrians were expanding their empire by invading the small countries lying between Assyria and Egypt, had encircled both Israel and Judah, and probably had demanded tribute from both. In 734 Israel and Syria, its northern neighbor, formed an anti-Assyrian alliance and attacked Ahaz, king of Judah, when he refused to join it. This invasion—the Syro-Ephraimitic War—was mentioned in the discussion of the date of the ministry of Hosea. Ahaz asked for Assyrian help, the last thing he really needed to seek. The Assyrians responded, crushing the allies swiftly and reducing Israel to a small city state. Ahaz then declared his loyalty to Assyria. This required him to replace the altar to Yahweh in the Temple in Jerusalem with an altar to the god of Assyria (2 Kings 16:5-18).

Shortly after the death of Tiglath-pileser III and before Shalmaneser V had grasped power in Assyria firmly, there was another revolt among the vassal states. The now badly weakened northern kingdom took part. Judah, the southern kingdom, remained faithful to Assyria. Shalmaneser V invaded Israel, destroyed all Israelite military forces in the field, occupied the land, and besieged the capital Samaria. The city held out for three years, its defenders hoping that Yahweh would come to their aid. It fell in 721 B.C. to Sargon, Shalmaneser's successor. Israel became an Assyrian province. Its leaders were deported and replaced with foreigners.

Unrest flared up spasmodically during the next sixteen years, often encouraged by the Egyptians, who understood the Assyrian menace quite well. The next major revolt broke out in 701 B.C. Sargon died, and before his successor could consolidate his power, a revolt broke out all across the empire. The governor of the large province of Babylonia may have started it (see 2 Kings 20:12-15), and all the small countries along the Mediterranean except Gaza and Ashdod, two Philistine city states, joined. Hezekiah, king of Judah, was one of the rebels. We saw earlier what happened to him. Sennacherib, the new Assyrian ruler, was as great a commander as his prececessors. He first crushed the revolt in Babylonia and then turned on the small countries along the Mediterranean. Judah collapsed before the Assyrian army and paid heavy tribute.

The ministry of Isaiah thus differed from the ministries of Amos and Hosea in at least one significant way. The first two prophets saw disaster looming in the future, but men could still argue that they were wrong. Isaiah worked during a catastrophe. All that he did and said must be understood against the background of the events through which he and his contemporaries were living.

When we seek in Isaiah traces of the ancient Shechem covenant renewal festival, we discover another difference. The only reference in chapters 1 to 39 to the enslavement in Egypt, the exodus, or the wilderness wanderings is Isaiah 10:24-26, the work of a disciple. The Egyptians of Isaiah's day were involved in some of the revolts against Assyria that he witnessed, and he mentions them for this reason (Is. 30:2-5; 31:1-3). He either ignored, or was ignorant of, the ancient saving history which Amos and Hosea held to be so important. He does seem, however, to have known the terms of the royal covenant recited at Shechem.

Deuteronomy 27:15 = Isaiah 2:8, 20
Deuteronomy 27:16 = Isaiah 3:5, 12
Deuteronomy 27:19 = Isaiah 1:17, 23; 10:1-2
Deuteronomy 27:25 = Isaiah 1:21-23

Gerhard von Rad has suggested that Isaiah believed in a tradition in which Yahweh's saving action is related to his defense of the holy mountain, Mount Zion.[8] It is true that there are many references both to Zion and to a holy mountain in the words of this prophet. References to Jerusalem should be listed here also, since Jerusalem is often said to be Zion. Important passages in which the prophet used this tradition are Isaiah 2:2-4—chapters 2-4 are a collection of oracles using various parts of the Mount Zion theme—10:27-34; 14:24-27, 28-32; 17:12-14; 18:1-7; 28:7-22; 29:1-8; 30:27-33; 31:1-8. All these reflect part, or all, of a Zion tradition also reported for us in Psalms 46, 48, 76, 99, 102:12-22.

An important part of the Mount Zion tradition was the belief that God would defend his holy city when it was in danger. This appears both in the Psalms and in the passages from Isaiah listed above. In Isaiah's lifetime, Jerusalem had been attacked twice, and the country for which it was the capital city had been in a state of constant danger. When the Syro-Ephraimitic alliance attacked in 734 B.C., Isaiah urged the king in Jerusalem to be calm (Is. 7:1-9). Could the reason for this be that Isaiah felt that Yahweh would defend his holy city himself? Was this same confidence the reason that the prophet was so sure that Assyria eventually would be destroyed (Is. 10:5-19)? What, then, is the significance of Isaiah 1:4-9?

> 4) Ah, sinful nation,
>   a people laden with iniquity,
>   offspring of evildoers,
>   sons who deal corruptly!
>   They have forsaken the LORD,
>   they have despised the Holy One of Israel,
>   they are utterly estranged.
> 5) Why will you still be smitten,
>   that you continue to rebel?
>   The whole head is sick,
>   and the whole heart faint.
> 6) From the sole of the foot even to the
>   head,
>   there is no soundness in it,
>   but bruises and sores
>   and bleeding wounds;
>   they are not pressed out, or bound up,
>   or softened with oil.

> 7) Your country lies desolate,
>   your cities are burned with fire;
>   in your very presence
>   aliens devour your land;
>   it is desolate, as overthrown by aliens.
> 8) And the daughter of Zion is left
>   like a booth in a vineyard,
>   like a lodge in a cucumber field,
>   like a besieged city.
> 9) If the LORD of hosts
>   had not left us a few survivors,
>   we should have been like Sodom,
>   and become like Gomorrah.

Here, Isaiah described the devastation of Judah after the Assyrian invasion of 701 B.C. without any hint of confidence that Jerusalem could not be captured. Popular legend, now preserved in 2 Kings 19:6-7, 21-34 (also in Is. 37:22-35) claimed that Isaiah had always been sure that Jerusalem could not be captured. Have we reason to question the popular legend?

The record of Isaiah becoming a prophet is reported in Isaiah 6:1-13. Verses 9-13 disturb us—especially verses 9 and 10.

> 9) And he said, "Go, and say to this people:
>   'Hear and hear, but do not understand;
>   see and see, but do not perceive.'
> 10) Make the heart of this people fat,
>   and their ears heavy,
>   and shut their eyes;
>   lest they see with their eyes,
>   and hear with their ears,
>   and understand with their hearts,
>   and turn and be healed."

Isaiah felt that he had been called to proclaim a message which was to deceive people into continuing to sin. This, on the face of it, is so fantastic that some explanation is needed.

We have already seen how Amos insisted that the royal freedom and power that enabled Yahweh to save also made it possible for him to punish, and how Hosea became convinced that any mercy Yahweh might show his people would arise out of his punishment of them. Is it possible to see in Isaiah's refusal to appeal to the Zion tradition in Isaiah 1:4-9, and in the strange theme of Isaiah 6:9-13, a new tradition the great prophets were slowly creating? Could Isaiah have come to feel that the rebellion of the Israelites was so serious that their punishment was a necessary prelude to any future act of blessing? Could he continue to believe that Yahweh would once again act on behalf of his people at the same time that he was convinced that the immediate future was to be punishment? If this were the case, was Isaiah saying that the disasters we experience are a part of salvation history?

There is another way to approach Isaiah's message of judgment. The ancient Israelites believed that their kings had a special status before God. They were the "anointed ones," that is, they were messiahs (see, for references to Saul as messiah: 1 Sam. 12:3, 5; 24:10; for references to David as messiah: 2 Sam. 22:51; Ps. 18:50). When Amos was accused of predicting the death of the king (Amos 7:10-11), he was being charged both with treason and blasphemy, yet he is pictured as accepting the accusation. Hosea openly attacked the monarchy. Once he charged the Israelites with having sinned from the beginning of the monarchy (Hos. 10:9). Gibeah, the village named here, was Saul's home and the first capital of the monarchy. Once Hosea described the monarchy itself as an expression of God's wrath (Hos. 13:9-11).

When Isaiah used the Zion, rather than the Shechem, tradition, he spoke as a true Jerusalemite. Zion was Jeruslaem, and the sacred traditions speaking of Mount Zion had come to be used by the kings of Jerusalem as a part of the royal ideology. Psalm 132 is part of a liturgy which once celebrated God's promise that the Davidic dynasty would rule forever. Notice verses 13-18.

> 13) For the LORD has chosen Zion;
>   he has desired it for his habitation:

14) "This is my resting place for ever;
     here I will dwell, for I have desired it.
15) I will abundantly bless her provisions;
     I will satisfy her poor with bread.
16) Her priests I will clothe with salvation,
     and her saints will shout for joy.
17) There I will make a horn to sprout for David;
     I have prepared a lamp for my anointed.
18) His enemies I will clothe with shame,
     but upon himself his crown will shed its luster."

When Isaiah accepted the Zion tradition, one might have expected him also to accept the view of the monarchy it contained. But he was a prophet first and a Jerusalemite second.

His call to become a prophet began with a shocking discovery. "In the year that King Uzziah died," he had a vision in which he saw the King, Yahweh Sabaoth (Is. 6:1-5), and he remained faithful to this vision throughout his life. He dismissed the royal court as rebels and thieves (Is. 1:23). God distinguished between the princely oppressors and the oppressed, and only the latter could be his people (Is. 3:13-15). In spite of the bite of Isaiah's attacks on injustice and misrule (see, for example Is. 5:8-25), the most vivid of Isaiah's words on this subject are given us in the form of a conversation between the prophet and King Ahaz.

(2) When the house of David was told, "Syria is in league with Ephraim," his heart and the heart of his people shook as the trees of the forest shake before the wind. (3) And the LORD said to Isaiah, "Go forth to meet Ahaz, you and Shear-jashub your son, at the end of the conduit of the upper pool on the highway to the Fuller's Field, (4) and say to him, 'Take heed, be quiet, do not fear, and do not let your heart be faint because of these two smoldering stumps of firebrands, at the fierce anger of Rezin and Syria and the son of Remaliah.' . . . (11) Ask a sign of the LORD your God; let it be as deep as Sheol or high as heaven." (12) But Ahaz said, "I will not ask, and I will not put the LORD to the test." (13) And he said, "Hear then, O house

of David! Is it too little for you to weary men, that you weary my God also?" (Is. 7:2-4, 11-13.)

Notice the shift in the possessive pronouns used in the latter half of the quotation. It is clear that Isaiah shared his fellow prophets' dislike for the abuses perpetrated by the royal court. He did not use the Zion tradition as the royal theologians did. It was not for him a source of optimism about the country and its king.

Instead, Isaiah saw the troubled present as the part of the Zion tradition in which the nations gathered to destroy the holy people and the holy city—but with one alarming change. Yahweh himself was summoning the enemy. It was,

> 5) Ah, Assyria, the rod of my anger,
>   the staff of my fury!
> 6) Against a godless nation I send him,
>   and against the people of my wrath I command
>   him,
> to take spoil and seize plunder,
>   and to tread them down like the mire of the
>   streets.   (Is. 10:5-6.)

Only after the faithless "holy people" had been winnowed by its enemies (Is. 6:9-13) and had lost all confidence in itself and in the false gods it trusted, would Yahweh step in on its behalf.

> 1) Ho Ariel, Ariel,
>   the city where David encamped!
> Add year to year;
>   let the feasts run their round.
> 2) Yet I will distress Ariel,
>   and there shall be moaning and lamentation,
>   and she shall be to me like an Ariel.
> 3) And I will encamp against you round about,
>   and will besiege you with towers
>   and I will raise siegeworks against you.
> 4) Then deep from the earth you shall speak,
>   from low in the dust your words shall come;

111

> your voice shall come from the ground like the
> > voice of a ghost,
> > and your speech shall whisper out of the dust.
> 5) But the multitude of your foes shall be like
> > small dust,
> > and the multitude of the ruthless like passing
> > chaff.
> And in an instant, suddenly,
> 6) you will be visited by the LORD of hosts
> > with thunder and with earthquake and great noise,
> > with whirlwind and tempest, and the flame of a
> > devouring fire.
> 7) And the multitude of all the nations that fight
> > against Ariel,
> > all that fight against her and her stronghold
> > and distress her,
> > shall be like a dream, a vision of the night.
> 8) As when a hungry man dreams he is eating
> > and awakes with his hunger not satisfied,
> > or as when a thirsty man dreams he is drinking
> > and awakes faint, with his thirst not quenched,
> > so shall the multitude of all the nations be
> > that fight against Mount Zion.
> > > > (Is. 29:1-8.)

Thus in Isaiah, as earlier in Amos, a great and ancient cultic tradition used to express the optimism of an idolatrous people was turned around and became the means for proclaiming anew the royal authority of Yahweh. He alone ruled Israel, and only obedience to his will was righteousness.

JEREMIAH

If we date the end of Isaiah's work about 700 B.C., seventy-four years passed before Jeremiah, Isaiah's successor, appeared. [9]

Jeremiah became a prophet in 626 B.C., thirteen years after Josiah came to the throne (Jer. 1:2). His ministry extended through the final siege, capture, and destruction of Jerusalem in 586 B.C. (Jer. 39:1-14). It thus lasted through the Wagnerian climax of the historical tragedy of the Judaean monarchy. When Jeremiah became a prophet, the court in Jerusalem was coming to the end of its long acceptance of a pro-Assyrian foreign policy. In 621 Josiah declared Judah to be independent of Assyria and cleansed the religion of the land of foreign practices. This was the great Deuteronomic reformation based on the law code in the book of Deuteronomy. The tiny kingdom was independent for twelve years. In 609 the Egyptians joined forces with their former conquerors, the Assyrians, to try to prevent the Babylonians from defeating the Assyrians completely and inheriting their empire. The Egyptian motive was probably the desire to capture for Egypt the southwestern part of the crumbling empire. Pharaoh Necho marched north to join the Assyrians and found his passage challenged by King Josiah and the army of Judah. You can predict the result. Josiah was killed, and his heir Jehoahaz, was deposed from the throne in Jerusalem by the Egyptians when they returned from a defeat in the north. Jehoahaz was replaced by Jehoiakim, his brother, who reigned as an Egyptian subject prince.

Jehoiakim later changed sides when it became clear that the power of Babylonia was the "wave of the future," but he revolted against his new masters in 598 B.C. The Babylonians invaded Judah, besieged and captured Jerusalem. Jehoiakim had died during the siege, and the Babylonians received the surrender of the city from a new king, Jehoiachin, who had been innocent of revolt. Jehoiachin was taken to Babylonia and maintained there by the Babylonians under house arrest as the legitimate heir to the throne in Jerusalem. Royal accounting records in Babylonia have been discovered which describe the provisions for Jehoiachin's support,[10] and the Old Testament tells us that he was set free and made a member of the Babylonian court thirty-seven years after his capture (2 Kings 25:27-30).

Zedekiah, an uncle of Jehoiachin, was placed on the throne in Jerusalem as the Babylonian puppet. He ruled obediently for a few years, but he finally refused to pay tribute in 586 B.C. The Babylonians invaded again; took Jerusalem by storm; destroyed its walls, palaces, and the Temple; and killed Zedekiah. Judah became a Babylonian province ruled from Mizpeh, and many of the nobility and craftsmen were taken away to Babylonia. The style and temperament of Isaiah and Jeremiah differ, but they were alike in two respects: both prophesied during catastrophe, and neither can be understood except in terms of their responses to disaster.

We have more information about Jeremiah than about any of the earlier great prophets. No school preserved his oracles. Instead, he had a secretary who recorded them and became such a devoted personal follower that he added his own account of the prophet's ministry to a collection of the prophet's words. The secretary's "biography" is to be found in those parts of chapters 26 through 45, where the prophet is spoken of in the third person. The results of the attempt to merge Yahwism and Baalism had, by Jeremiah's time, begun to influence the course of the prophet's life. We do not know whether Amos, Hosea, or Isaiah had been persecuted —although Amos 7:10-17 sets the stage for persecution—but we do know that Jeremiah was put in the stocks (Jer. 19:14–20:6), tried for blasphemy and treason (Jer. 26), imprisoned for an alleged attempt to desert to the enemy (Jer. 37:11-21), and tried for subversion (Jer. 38:1-13). Since we have only one reference to personal troubles endured by earlier prophets (Jer. 26:17-23), we have some reason for suspecting that Jeremiah's persecutions were unique. They may have reflected a disintegration in the life of the nation which included contempt for spokesmen of the nation's God.

Statements are preserved from Jeremiah which we cannot imagine his predecessors making. Compare the terse dignity of Amos' description of why he had become a prophet (Amos 7:14-15) with the uncertainty and suffering reported by Jeremiah.

> 14) Cursed be the day
> on which I was born!

The day when my mother bore me,
   let it not be blessed!
15) Cursed be the man
      who brought the news to my father,
   "A son is born to you,"
      making him very glad.
16) Let that man be like the cities
      which the LORD overthrew without pity;
   let him hear a cry in the morning
      and an alarm at noon,
17) because he did not kill me in the womb;
      so my mother would have been my grave,
      and her womb for ever great.
(18) Why did I come forth from the womb
      to see toil and sorrow,
      and spend my days in shame?
                        (Jer. 20:14-18.) [11]

This may be only Jeremiah's reaction to his suffering. It is probable, however, that doubt about his standing as a prophet intensified his sufferings. Jeremiah had the misfortune to be a spokesman for Yahweh at a time when the leaders of the people cared so little about the Lord that they felt free to persecute his spokesmen. God's spokesman himself felt so unsure of his calling to be a spokesman that he was tormented by his own doubts. It sounds strangely modern, does it not?

Each of the great prophets was great for more than one reason, and our study of them here obviously is incomplete. We have been trying to understand only how the work of these men fits into the pattern already seen in our discussion of the history of salvation. We will begin our examination of Jeremiah's message where we started in the study of Amos, Hosea, and Isaiah, by asking how many hints we can find of the ancient history of salvation associated with the Shechemite festival for the renewal of the covenant.

As soon as we look for references, we begin to find them. Jeremiah 2:6; 11:4, 7; 31:32; 32:20-23 mention the exodus. The wanderings in the wilderness are mentioned in Jeremiah 2:2, 6. The invasion of Canaan is recalled in Jeremiah 2:7. The prophet also spoke frequently of the kind of themes associated with the curses used in the Shechemite festival and found in Deuteronomy.

Deuteronomy 27:15 = Jeremiah 2:27-28; 8:19
Deuteronomy 27:19 = Jeremiah 5:1, 28
Deuteronomy 27:20-23 = Jeremiah 2:23-25; 3:2; 5:7-8
Deuteronomy 27:24 = Jeremiah 5:26-28; 9:3-5; 21:12
Deuteronomy 27:25 = Jeremiah 2:34; 5:1-2.
Deuteronomy 27:26 = Jeremiah 5:4-5; 6:16-18; 8:7; 26:4-5;
　　35:16

We can say confidently that Jeremiah—like Amos and Hosea—knew and accepted the traditions of the ancient Shechemite covenant festival.

Jeremiah's importance begins to emerge when the following statements are considered together. He shared the same tradition that was the basis for the book of Deuteronomy, and he lived during the reformation of Josiah which was based on Deuteronomy; yet at some point in his life he declared,

> How can you say, "We are wise,
> 　and the law of the LORD is with us"?
> But, behold, the false pen of the scribes
> 　has made it into a lie.
>
> 　　　　　　　　　　　　(Jer. 8:8.)

These words almost certainly refer to the Deuteronomic reformation. The first two statements suggest that Jeremiah would have supported the reformation. The third indicates that he questioned it at some time in his life. Is it possible to explain why the prophet opposed a reformation based on a law code derived from the same cultic tradition in which he himself stood?

The problem of Jeremiah's relationship to the Deuteronomic reformation has been debated vigorously by scholars and may never be settled to everyone's satisfaction. Four positions have been defended: that Jeremiah supported the reformation, that he began by supporting it but became disillusioned and later opposed it, that he always opposed it, and that his ministry did not begin until after the reformation was over. The verse just quoted has always been quoted by those holding either the second or the third of the four positions. A choice between these two has been based upon a study of two other passages.

Jeremiah 7:1–8:12 and 11:1-7 are the clearest references to the Deuteronomic reformation in the book of Jeremiah. Although the Deuteronomic School wrote in a style that is distinctive when seen against the background of the whole of the Old Testament, it seems actually to have been just good Hebrew in the age in which it was written. Both Jeremiah and Baruch, his secretary, lived in this same era, and Baruch's style is very close to the style used by the Deuteronomists. It is very difficult therefore to decide whether some parts of the book of Jeremiah are the work of Baruch reporting Jeremiah, or the work of the Deuteronomic School editing the book of Jeremiah. The problem is serious because Jeremiah 7:1–8:3 (minus 7:29. Jer. 7:29 and 8:4-12 are in the style of Jeremiah) have the kind of style just described. Who wrote these verses, Baruch or the Deuteronomists? If Baruch, Jeremiah probably did support the reformation at some time in his ministry; if the Deuteronomists, then Jeremiah may never have supported the reformation since there would seem to have been need to manufacture evidence claiming that he had. Jeremiah 7:29 and 8:4-12, the verses which clearly are from Jeremiah, are condemnation.

This is the kind of problem which literary criticism is expected to solve, and literary critics have done brilliant and detailed work on it. Unfortunately, no set of conclusions has gained wide acceptance. The Deuteronomic "style" seems to be too close to the style of the era to which the Deuteronomists, Jeremiah, and Baruch all belonged. The only way we can reach a decision between the possibilities is on the basis of our understanding of other passages in the book of Jeremiah.

One such passage is Jeremiah 2:2-3.

2) "Go and proclaim in the hearing of Jerusalem,
    Thus says the LORD,
  I remember the devotion of your youth,
    your love as a bride,
  how you followed me in the wilderness,
    in a land not sown.
3) Israel was holy to the LORD,
    the first fruits of his harvest.
  All who ate of it became guilty;
    evil came upon them,
                                says the LORD."

This passage stands by itself because Jeremiah 2:4 begins a new oracle. It therefore should be studied by itself. When this is done, the two verses quoted above are found to be encouragement. Yahweh is telling the men of Jerusalem that he is remembering how faithful they had been during their wanderings in the wilderness—rather than their more recent sins—and how he defended them then from their enemies—not how he has been punishing them through their enemies more recently. When would such encouragement be proper during Jeremiah's lifetime? Only when the people were trying to return to sacred traditions which told of their faithfulness during their wilderness wanderings—as during the Deuteronomic reformation—and only when the nation was independent and worshiping only Yahweh—as during the years when the Deuteronomic reformation was in force. Thus Jeremiah's support of the reformation gives us a proper background for this oracle.

Having reason now to believe that there is evidence in Jeremiah's own words both for his support of the reformation and for his opposition to it, we can assign Jeremiah 7:1-15 and 11:1-8 to Baruch with some confidence. Both passages fit what we already know of the prophet's ministry, and we can use the additional details they supply.

A fairly complete story can now be traced. Jeremiah 11:1-8 reflects a period when Jeremiah supported the reformation. "And the LORD said to me, 'Proclaim all these words in the cities of Judah, and in the streets of Jerusalem: Hear the words of this covenant and do them.'" (Vs. 6.) Jeremiah 7:1-15, however, reports the prophet's uneasiness. The people seemed to feel that it was enough to chant, "The temple of the LORD, the temple of the LORD, the temple of the LORD" (vs. 4). Jeremiah understood the reformation to require basic changes in attitude and conduct.

(5) For if you truly amend your ways and your doings, if you truly execute justice one with another, (6) if you do not oppress the alien, the fatherless or the widow, or shed innocent blood in this place, and if you do not go after other gods to your own hurt, (7) then I will let you dwell in this place, in the land that I gave of old to your fathers for ever. (Jer. 7:5-7.)

Verses 8-15 then expand the contrast found in Jeremiah 7:4-7 between popular piety and the prophet's understanding of God's will. Jeremiah 7:16–8:3 and 11:9-17 report the same situation. The prophet was convinced that the reformation had been so debased that it had become merely another form of rebellion against God's will. His contemporaries had had an opportunity to repent, but they would not, just as their fathers had had the chance to serve God but chose rather to serve the baals. The prophet is ordered not to pray for his people. The reformation had failed.

The main themes of Jeremiah's ministry fit well into the view of his relationship to the reformation just given. We have already seen that Jeremiah accepted the same cultic traditions as those reflected in Deuteronomy. He also had much the same outlook as had the members of the Deuteronomic School. The offense of Israel was that it had rejected its bond with Yahweh.

> 5) Thus says the LORD:
>> "What wrong did your fathers find in me
>>> that they went far from me,
>> and went after worthlessness, and became
>>> worthless?

6) They did not say, 'Where is the LORD
   who brought us up from the land of Egypt,
   who led us in the wilderness,
       in a land of deserts and pits,
   in a land of drought and deep darkness,
       in a land that none passes through,
           where no man dwells?'
7) And I brought you into a plentiful land
       to enjoy its fruits and its good things.
   But when you came in you defiled my land,
       and made my heritage an abomination."

                                          (Jer. 2:5-7.)

The rejection of Yahweh took the form of a cult after the
Canaanite pattern which involved ritual promiscuity (Jer. 2:23–
3:5, 13; 5:7-8; 13:27), cultic lamentation for the dying-rising
savior god (Jer. 3:21), making and sacrificing fertility symbols
(Jer. 7:18), the use of figurines of the gods (Jer. 8:19), and
the sacrifice of the firstborn (Jer. 7:31)—and with it all the
abandonment of the ancient command to do justice and mercy, so
that,

> Heaping oppression upon oppression,
>   and deceit upon deceit,
>   they refuse to know me, says the LORD.
>   (Jer. 9:6.)

When the people had the opportunity to repent, to change from
their false worship to a purer worship of Yahweh under the
guidance of the Deuteronomic Code, the leadership of Josiah, and
the urging of the prophets, they gave only lip service to the reform.
Beneath the use of a few correct phrases lurked the ancient
paganism of a rebellious people.

> 4) You shall say to them, Thus says the LORD:
>   When men fall, do they not rise again?
>   If one turns away, does he not return?

5) Why then has this people turned away
in perpetual backsliding?
They hold fast to deceit,
they refuse to return.
6) I have given heed and listened,
but they have not spoken aright;
no man repents of his wickedness,
saying, "What have I done?"
Every one turns to his own course,
like a horse plunging headlong into battle.
7) Even the stork in the heavens
knows her times;
and the turtledove, swallow, and crane
keep the time of their coming;
but my people know not
the ordinance of the LORD.

(Jer. 8:4-7.)

At some point Jeremiah became so desperate that he cried,

Can the Ethiopian change his skin
or the leopard his spots?
Then also you can do good
who are accustomed to do evil.

(Jer. 13:23.)

All Israelites were involved, but especially the royal court (Jer. 22:13-19) and the religious leaders (Jer. 8:8-12; 23:9-22), prophet and priest alike (Jer. 6:13).

The only future Jeremiah could see for such a rebellious people was a storm of divine wrath, yet he seems to have found it impossible to proclaim it without deep but hidden anguish.

15) Hear and give ear; be not proud,
for the LORD has spoken.
16) Give glory to the LORD your God
before he brings darkness,
before your feet stumble

> on the twilight mountains,
> and while you look for light
> he turns it into gloom
> and makes it deep darkness.
> 17) But if you will not listen,
> my soul will weep in secret for your
> pride;
> my eyes will weep bitterly and run down
> with tears,
> because the LORD's flock has been taken
> captive.
> (Jer. 13:15-17; see also 8:22–9:3.)

An even deeper tragedy awaited the prophet. It is possible to derive some desperate comfort from the proclamation of a message of doom if one is convinced that it is a true message. Even this slender comfort is stripped from the spokesman for disaster who fears that he may have been deceived. Jeremiah's ministry spanned the entire Deuteronomic reformation. He witnessed the death of Josiah, the royal sponsor of the reformation, and the prophet's high regard for the king has been preserved for us in Jeremiah's condemnation of the son.

> 15) Do you think you are a king
> because you compete in cedar?
> Did not your father eat and drink
> and do justice and righteousness?
> Then it was well with him.
> 16) He judged the cause of the poor and needy;
> then it was well.
> Is not this to know me?
> says the LORD.
> (Jer. 22:15-16.)

Jeremiah, like the members of the Deuteronomic School, was a child of his culture. It seemed obvious to him that righteousness brought divine reward and wickedness brought divine wrath. Life was reward; death was wrath. When Josiah died in battle defending the independence of the people of God, he reaped wrath for his righteousness. How did Jeremiah respond?

The death of Josiah is not mentioned in the book of Jeremiah. There are, however, a series of oracles in which the prophet voices a despair so intense that it must be let speak for itself.

> 7) O LORD, thou hast deceived me,
>   and I was deceived;
>   thou art stronger than I,
>   and thou hast prevailed.
>   I have become a laughingstock all the day;
>   everyone mocks me.
> 8) For whenever I speak, I cry out,
>   I shout, "Violence and destruction!"
>   For the word of the LORD has become for me
>   a reproach and derision all day long.
> 9) If I say, "I will not mention him,
>   or speak any more in his name,"
>   there is in my heart as it were a burning
>   fire
>   shut up in my bones,
>   and I am weary with holding it in,
>   and I cannot.
>   (Jer. 20:7-9; see also 20:14-18.)

Yet it was Jeremiah who proclaimed a hope for a new covenant.

(31) Behold, the days are coming, says the LORD, when I will make a new covenant with the house of Israel and the house of Judah, (32) not like the covenant which I made with their fathers when I took them by the hand to bring them out of the land of Egypt, my covenant which they broke, though I was their husband, says the LORD. (33) But this is the covenant which I will make with the house of Israel after those days, says the LORD: I will put my law within them, and I will write it upon their hearts; and I will be their God, and they shall be my people. (34) And no longer shall each man teach his neighbor and each his brother, saying, "Know the LORD," for they shall all know me, from the least of them to the greatest, says the LORD; for I will forgive their

123

iniquity, and I will remember their sin no more. (Jer. 31:31-34; see also 4:3-4.)

Jeremiah believed that life would go on in Palestine even after the defeat of the nation and the capture of Jerusalem. During the siege of the city he bought land offered him by his uncle in order to keep it in the family (Jer. 32:6-12) because God had commanded him to do so as a sign of promise.

(14) Thus says the LORD of hosts, the God of Israel: Take these deeds, both this sealed deed of purchase and this open deed, and put them in an earthenware vessel, that they may last for a long time. (15) For thus says the LORD of hosts, the God of Israel: Houses and fields and vineyards shall again be bought in this land. (Jer. 32:14-15.)

It is difficult to avoid the suspicion that God chose once more to speak to a prophet in the midst of the prophet's agony, proclaiming to him and though him a great new theme.

NOTES

1. Isaiah, Jeremiah, Ezekiel, Hosea, Joel, Amos, Obadiah, Micah, Nahum, Habakkuk, Zephaniah, Haggai, Zechariah, Malachi. This list agrees with neither the Jewish nor the traditional Christian grouping. The Hebrew Bible puts all these except the first three into one book (which includes Jonah) called the Book of the Twelve. Traditional Christian usage separates the Book of the Twelve into twelve books and adds the book of Daniel to get the Minor Prophets. Neither Jonah nor Daniel appears in the list given here. Jonah is an enlarged prophetic parable. Daniel is apocalypse, not prophecy.
2. Several useful books deal with the prophets as a whole, and their relevant chapters should be consulted in the study of individual prophets. The most comprehensive is Johannes Lindblom, *Prophecy in Ancient Israel* (Philadelphia: Muhlenberg Press, 1962). See also R. B. Y. Scott, *The Relevance of the Prophets* (New York: The Macmillan Company, 1944); J. M. P. Smith, *The Prophets and Their Times;* John Paterson, *The Goodly Fellowship of the Prophets: Studies Historical, Religious and Expository in the Hebrew Prophets* (New York: Charles Scribner's Sons, 1948).
3. Verse-by-verse studies of a biblical book are called commentaries. They

provide the most detailed study helps available, but they vary in thoroughness and in the kinds of research methods used in their preparation. There is in print as of this date no thorough recent commentary on Amos in English. Four older commentaries—all using literary and historical criticism only—are available. The two most detailed are W. R. Harper, *A Critical and Exegetical Commentary on the Books of Amos and Hosea* (New York: Charles Scribner's Sons, 1905), and R. S. A. Cripps, *A Critical and Exegetical Commentary on the Book of Amos* ([New York: The Macmillan Co., 1929] Napierville: Alec R. Allenson, 1955). Briefer but still reliable older commentaries are S. R. Driver, *The Books of Joel and Amos, with Introduction and Notes* ("Cambridge Bible for Schools and Colleges" [Cambridge: Cambridge University Press, 1898]), and J. M. P. Smith, *A Commentary on the Books of Amos, Hosea and Micah* ("The Bible for Home and School" [New York: The Macmillan Company, 1914]). A recent brief commentary depending heavily on insights derived from archaeology is Jacob M. Myers, *Hosea, Joel, Amos, Obediah and Jonah,* ("The Layman's Bible Commentary" [Richmond: John Knox Press, 1959]). Two books which are not commentaries should be mentioned: R. E. Wolfe, *Meet Amos and Hosea, the Prophets of Israel* (New York: Harper & Brothers, 1945), is a biographical approach; A. S. Kapelrud, *Central Ideas in Amos* (Oslo: W. Nygaard, 1956), is a patternist approach.

4. For brief descriptions of Canaanite religion, see John Gray, "Baal (Deity)," *The Interpreter's Dictionary of the Bible;* and G. E. Wright, "Baalism," *An Encyclopedia of Religion,* Vergilius Ferm, ed. (New York: The Philosophical Library, 1945), pp. 51-52. For more detailed studies, see A. S. Kapelrud, *Baal in the Ras Shamra Texts* (Copenhagen: G. E. C. Gad, 1952); G. R. Driver, *Canaanite Myths and Legends from Ugarit* (Edinburgh: T. & T. Clark, 1956); Cyrus H. Gordon, *The Loves and Wars of Baal and Anat, and Other Poems from Ugarit* (Princeton: Princeton University Press, 1943); Julian Obermann, *Ugaritic Mythology* (New Haven: Yale University Press, 1948); and T. Gaster, *Thespis: Ritual, Myth and Drama in the Ancient Near East.*

5. Consult works in Note 3 which include Hosea in their titles. For a detailed commentary using literary and historical criticism, see S. L. Brown, *The Book of Hosea, with Introduction and Notes* (London: Methuen & Co., 1932); James M. Ward, *Hosea: A Theological Commentary* (New York: Harper & Row, 1966), uses some form criticism and patternism in addition to literary and historical criticism. G. A. F. Knight, *Hosea, Introduction and Commentary* (London: SCM Press, 1960), is recent but brief. H. Wheeler Robinson, *The Cross of Hosea* (Philadelphia: The Westminster Press, 1949), is a sensitively Christian discussion of the message of Hosea.

6. The Hebrew text here reads "Judah," but I have accepted the view that the structure of the poetry suggests "Israel" as the original.

7. The best of the detailed older commentaries on Isaiah 1–39 are: G. B. Gray, *A Critical and Exegetical Commentary on the Book of Isaiah I-XXXIX* (New York: Charles Scribner's Sons, 1912), and G. H. Box, *The Book of Isaiah* (London: Isaac Pitman and Sons, 1908). Older shorter commentaries are: J. E. McFadyen, *The Book of the Prophecies of Isaiah* ("Bible for Home and School" [New York: The Macmillan Company, 1910]), John Skinner, *The Book of the Prophet Isaiah, with Introduction and Notes* ("The Cambridge Bible for Schools and College" [Cambridge: Cambridge University Press, 1897/98]). More recent but also less detailed: R. B. Y. Scott, "Isaiah 1–39; Introduction and Exegesis," *The Interpreter's Bible*, V, 151-381. E. A. Leslie's *Isaiah, Chronologically Arranged, Translated and Interpreted* (Nashville: Abingdon Press, 1963) reflects the use of literary, historical, and form criticism but suffers from lack of explanation of the scholarly decisions made. Sheldon H. Blank, *Prophetic Faith in Isaiah* (New York: Harper & Brothers, 1958), is a statement of the message of the prophet by a great contemporary liberal Jewish scholar.

8. See G. von Rad, "The City on the Hill," in *The Problem of the Hexateuch and Other Essays*, pp. 214-24; and *Old Testament Theology*, Stalker, tr. (New York: Harper & Row, 1965), II, 155-69.

9. There are several recent commentaries in English on Jeremiah. The most detailed is John Bright, *Jeremiah, Introduction, Translation and Notes* ("The Anchor Bible" [Garden City: Doubleday & Company, 1965]), a work relying heavily on recent archaeological discoveries; E. A. Leslie, *Jeremiah, Chronologically Arranged, Translated and Interpreted* (Apex Books, Nashville: Abingdon Press, 1954), but see the comment in Note 7 above on the work on Isaiah by this same author; and J. P. Hyatt, "Jeremiah: Introduction and Exegesis," *The Interpreter's Bible*, V, 777-1142. Two less detailed recent commentaries also are available: H. Cunliffe-Jones, *The Book of Jeremiah: Introduction and Commentary* ("Torch Bible Commentaries" [London: SCM Press, 1960]); H. T. Kuist, *The Book of Jeremiah and the Lamentations of Jeremiah* ("The Layman's Bible Commentary" [Richmond: John Knox Press, 1960]), rather too conservative. H. Wheeler Robinson, *The Cross of Jeremiah* (London: SCM Press, 1925), is a work which is as sensitive and valuable as this scholar's similar work on Hosea. An excellent older study help is J. Skinner, *Prophecy and Religion: Studies in the Life of Jeremiah* (Cambridge: Cambridge University Press, 1922).

10. See Oppenheim, "Babylonian and Assyrian Historical Texts," in Pritchard, ed., *Ancient Near Eastern Texts*, p. 308*b*; and in *The Ancient Near East; an Anthology*, p. 205.

11. See also Jer. 11:18-23; 12:1-6 (less vs. 4); 15:10-21 (less vss. 13-14); 18:8-23; and 20:7-12.

V

THE EXILIC PROPHETS

EZEKIEL

The book of Ezekiel is the most difficult of the prophetic books to read, as well as the most difficult to study.[1] Ezekiel seems to have behaved insanely at times. Visions alternate with monotonous, wordy condemnations. Symbolic acts of incredible severity follow reports of experiences which are difficult to believe. The basic outlines of the book are clear. There are three main divisions: condemnations of Israel (chaps. 1-24), condemnations of foreign nations (chaps. 25–32), and predictions of the restoration of Israel (chaps. 33–48). It is unlikely that the oracles were given originally in their present order, but the threefold division of the book may reflect three stages in the prophet's ministry.

There are some details about his life. We are told that he was a priest and that he was among a group taken into exile in 598 B.C., the first time the Babylonians captured Jerusalem (Ezek. 1:1-3). Many of his oracles are dated, and these dates may be accurate.[2] We know that he was married, loved his wife, and became a widower (Ezek. 24:15-18). We are also told that the leaders of the exiles came to hear what he had to say—even if they did not heed what they heard (Ezek. 33:30-32). We know that his ministry began before the destruction of Jerusalem in 586 and continued among the exiles after that event (Ezek. 33:21-33).

It also is clear that Ezekiel knew a bewildering variety of traditions, some of which he describes more fully than any other writer in the Old Testament. Two of these, the creation myth and the myth of the garden of God, may have been parts of a single, larger whole.

We have already noted, in the discussion of Amos, that the ancient Semitic creation myth told of a conflict between a god of order and a god of chaos. The former deity was the salvation god; the latter was the deity of death. In the Old Testament, the chaos god was called Rahab, Leviathan, or the serpent (or dragon), and the kingdom of Leviathan was the abyss, sometimes equated with death and at other times with the ocean. Yahweh was the god of order, of salvation, of life. Notice how Ezekiel used the theme of the conflict between these gods to describe Yahweh's defeat of Egypt.

> 3) . . . Thus says the Lord GOD:
> "Behold, I am against you,
>   Pharaoh king of Egypt,
> the great dragon that lies
>   in the midst of his streams,
> that says, 'My Nile is my own;
>   I made it.'
> 4) I will put hooks in your jaws,
>   and make the fish of your streams stick
>   to your scales;
>   and I will draw you up out of the midst
>   of your streams,
>   with all the fish of your streams
>   which stick to your scales.
> 5) And I will cast you forth into the wilderness,
>   you and all the fish of your streams;
> you shall fall upon the open field,
>   and not be gathered and buried.
> To the beasts of the earth and to the birds
>   of the air
> I have given you as food."
> (Ezek. 29:3*b*-9; see also 32:2-8; 28:2-10.)

Another mythological theme was the garden of God. A tree of life is nourished by the waters of life. The waters then flow out into the rest of the earth to bring life to it. Each shrine using this myth had its own garden of God and its own tree of life. The king was the head of the cult, and he was often described as the caretaker of the garden. His scepter and his dynasty were sometimes said to be branches or roots of the tree, or vine, of life.[3]

This myth appears several times in Ezekiel. In Ezekiel 17:1-10 it was used as a condemnation of a Judean king, and in 19:10-14 it was applied to the queen mother in Jerusalem. More often, however, Ezekiel used it in his oracles against other nations. The myth of the garden of God appears in its fullest form in the Old Testament in Genesis 3 and Ezekiel 28:11-19. In the latter passage it is a part of the description of the downfall of the king of Tyre:

11) Moreover the word of the LORD came to me: 12) "Son of man, raise a lamentation over the king of Tyre, and say to him, Thus says the Lord GOD:

> "You were the signet of perfection,
> full of wisdom
> and perfect in beauty.
>
> 13) You were in Eden, in the garden of God;
> every precious stone was your covering,
> carnelian, topaz, and jasper,
> chrysolite, beryl, and onyx,
> sapphire, carbuncle, and emerald;
> and wrought in gold were your settings
> and your engravings.
> On the day that you were created
> they were prepared.
>
> 14) With an anointed guardian cherub I placed you;
> you were on the holy mountain of God;
> in the midst of the stones of fire you walked.
>
> 15) You were blameless in your ways
> from the day you were created,
> till iniquity was found in you.
>
> 16) In the abundance of your trade
> you were filled with violence, and you
> sinned;
> so I cast you as a profane thing from
> the mountain of God,

and the guardian cherub drove you out
from the midst of the stones of fire."
(Ezek. 28:11-16.)

The prophet used another part of the myth, the tree of life, in his description of the downfall of Egypt, and one part of this is especially interesting.

7) It was beautiful in its greatness,
   in the length of its branches;
  for its roots went down
   to abundant waters.
8) The cedars in the garden of God could
    not rival it,
   nor the fir trees equal its boughs;
  the plane trees were as nothing
   compared with its branches;
  no tree in the garden of God
   was like it in beauty.
9) I made it beautiful
   in the mass of its branches,
  and all the trees of Eden envied it,
   that were in the garden of God.
   (Ezek. 31:7-9; see also vss. 2-6.)

One of the problems of the study of the book of Ezekiel is the relationship of the three parts of the book. We can fit part one—condemnations of Judah and Israel—to part three—promises of the restoration of Yahweh's people—by saying that Ezekiel felt that the judgment he was predicting ended with the destruction of Jerusalem in 586 B.C. After 586 he turned to a message of hope to encourage the defeated people. This raises at least one serious question. The prophet insisted throughout part one that the covenant between Yahweh and Israel had ended. This freed Yahweh from any responsibility in the future toward Israel, and there would be no reason for him to restore Israel. A careful reader of part three would have another question. There is actually very little here which would make one think that Ezekiel was trying to encourage a defeated people. One has the feeling that he was speaking of an event far enough in the future that few, or none, of those hearing him would see it. Did he expect a wholly new Israel unrelated to the old Israel?

Even if we are willing to accept the interpretation of the relationship of parts one and three just given, part two does not fit. One explanation might be that the oracles against the foreign nations are simply vindictiveness. Some of those nations had helped Judah get into trouble; others were enemies of long standing. But this view of the unity of the book of Ezekiel gives us a view of the prophet that is unattractive, to say the least. According to it, he predicted the destruction of his nation until it happened. Then he reversed himself, encouraged the people experiencing the punishment he had predicted, and cursed the nation's enemies through whom the divinely ordered destruction had come. It is no wonder that some scholars have argued that large parts of the book are not the work of the prophet.

But there is a different way of understanding Ezekiel's message. It is built of three elements.

The first is Ezekiel's view of his nation's past. Ezekiel 20:1-44 makes it clear that the prophet knew the exodus tradition. These same verses also make it plain that he either knew it in a slightly different form than Jeremiah, or that he interpreted it differently. Jeremiah pictured the time of the wandering in the wilderness as a honeymoon and reminded his hearers of their forefathers' faithfulness (Jer. 2:2-3). Amos earlier had had nothing to say about the faithfulness or faithlessness of Israel at the beginning of its history—unless Amos 5:25 is such a reference—but he did assert that the faithlessness began early (Amos 2:10-12). Ezekiel believed that the faithlessness began even before Israel had been led out of Egypt.

(5b) Thus says the Lord GOD: On the day when I chose Israel, I swore to the seed of the house of Jacob, making myself known to them in the land of Egypt, I swore to them, saying, I am the LORD your God. (6) On that day I swore to them that I would bring them out of the land of Egypt into a land that I had searched out for them, a land flowing with milk and honey, the most glorious of all lands. (7) And I said to them, Cast away the detestable things your eyes feast on, every one of you, and do not defile yourselves with the idols of Egypt; I am the LORD your God. (8) But they rebelled against me and would not listen to me; they did not every man cast away the detestable things their eyes feasted on, nor did they forsake the idols of Egypt. (Ezek. 20:5*b*-8*a*.)

There had never been a time when this people had responded to Yahweh in faithfulness (see also vss. 13, 21, 28). Ezekiel recited the ancient salvation history in such a way that it was a history of rebellion.

The second element is Ezekiel's use of mythological themes. As you may have noticed, all the passages that have been examined dealt with judgment. Did you also notice that a strong contrast was either stated or implied in all these references? In every one, the strength of the person or group being destroyed is pictured in mythological terms while the destruction by Yahweh is given in historical terms.

We saw earlier that Amos reversed the mythological motif of the "day of the Lord" in his warning that Yahweh was about to punish a faithless people. In Isaiah's use of the myth of the mountain of God, he insisted that Yahweh would protect his holy mountain and holy city only after he had punished a faithless people. Jeremiah turned his back on the first serious attempt in a century to revive the ancient Shechemite tradition, after having supported it initially. In each of these cases, a prophet inverted a major cultic tradition. Now we see Ezekiel reinterpreting the ancient sacred history to make it a history of faithlessness, and using the myths preserved in the cult as statements of judgment rather than of salvation.

The third element is the reason given by the prophet for Yahweh's saving acts. The same motivation that worked in the past will work again in the future. The prophet's recital of the ancient saving history pictured God as saying:

(8*b*) Then I thought I would pour out my wrath upon them and spend my anger against them in the midst of the land of Egypt. (9) But I acted for the sake of my name, that it should not be profaned in the sight of the nations among whom they dwelt, in whose sight I made myself known to them in bringing them out of the land of Egypt. (Ezek. 20:8*b*, 9.)

As for the future:

(22) Therefore say to the house of Israel, Thus says the Lord God: It is not for your sake, O house of Israel, that I am about to act, but for the sake of my holy name, which you have profaned among the nations to which you came. (23) And I will vindicate the holiness of my great name, which has been profaned among the nations, and which you have profaned among them; and the nations will know that I am the Lord, says the Lord God, when through you I vindicate my holiness before their eyes. (24) For I will take you from the nations, and gather you from all the countries, and bring you into your own land. . . . (32) It is not for your own sake that I will act, says the Lord God; let that be known to you. Be ashamed and confounded for your ways, O house of Israel. (Ezek. 36:22-24, 32.)

It is difficult to judge Ezekiel's uniqueness. He was a priest and may have used sacred traditions which were less important to the other prophets. What seems to us to be distinctive in him may actually have been typical of the circles of which he was a part. This seems unlikely, however. We have just seen how he turned upside down every major cultic tradition which he used. In place of the familiar themes of a God acting out of love for his people, Ezekiel spoke of a God so aloof that he acted only out of consideration for his own reputation. He had chosen this people, and he would not admit that he had made a mistake.

Yet Ezekiel was entirely consistent. He was proclaiming a God so sovereign that he acted solely because of self-respect, a

God so sovereign that he would tolerate no human pretensions. Thus Ezekiel spoke of a God who was punishing his people for its faithlessness, humbling the foreign nations through whom he had executed his punishment of Israel, and restoring a helpless Israel —all in order to maintain his self-respect.

This is a chilling view of God, but Ezekiel labored during the climax of his nation's tragedy. Men needed a terrible insight in order to survive in a terrible hour. A God who merely loves satisfies the needs only of the comfortable. Ezekiel met the desperation of his generation by plumbing the depth in God which Martin Luther later also was to sense: the ultimate strangeness of God even though he chooses to approach men in love.

THE SECOND ISAIAH

It has already been pointed out that a study of the historical references in the book of Isaiah justifies the conclusion that we have here the records of the work of two great prophets and their disciples. The earlier prophet, Isaiah ben Amoz, worked from 740 to 700 B.C. The later prophet labored about 540, over a century and a half later. Isaiah 40–55 contains the words of the second of these prophets. His name is unknown to us—hence the title the Second Isaiah—but he was the greatest of the six great prophets.[4]

You will search these fifteen chapters for his name without finding it. It may be that Isaiah 50:4-9 is his description of his vocational call, but this is the only passage that might give us any personal information about him. He spoke plainly enough about the age in which he lived. If you will consult the chronological chart at the end of this chapter, you can see for yourself the significance of the evidence. Cyrus the Great is mentioned in such a way that it is clear that his rise to power has begun but is not ended (Is. 44:24–45:7). The defeat of Babylonia is close enough for a captive to urge his fellows to return home (Is. 48:20) and to speak plainly of Babylonia's defeat (Is. 47:1-15). Even the gods of Babylon are pictured as already defeated (Is.

46:1-2). This is an important statement when we remember that
men then believed that the victory or defeat of a nation was the
victory or defeat of its gods. All this information points to a date
close to the capture of Babylon by Cyrus the Great.

These chapters also reveal the mood of the prophet's fellow
captives. Their fathers had been warned repeatedly by earlier
prophets that the nation's conduct had caused Yahweh to end his
covenant with them. When defeat and captivity came, enough
Israelites accepted the prophets' interpretation as right to preserve
the prophets' words. It would not be strange that some of these
people, feeling that they now had no god, would begin looking
for a new god to worship. This seems to be the situation reflected
in some of the oracles of the Second Isaiah. He quoted the popular
view that the relationship between Yahweh and Israel had ended.

> Why do you say, O Jacob,
>   and speak, O Israel,
> "My way is hid from the Lord,
>   and my right is disregarded by my God"?
>   (Is. 40:27; see also 49:14; 50:1.)

But there were no other gods Israel could worship. The other
"gods" were not gods.

> 21) Set forth your case, says the Lord;
>   bring your proofs, says the King of Jacob.
> 22) Let them bring them, and tell us
>   what is to happen.
>   Tell us the former things, what they are,
>   that we may consider them,
>   that we may know their outcome;
>   or declare to us the things to come.
> 23) Tell us what is to come hereafter,
>   that we may know that you are gods;
>   do good, or do harm,
>   that we may be dismayed and terrified.
> 24) Behold, you are nothing,

and your work is nought;
an abomination is he who chooses you.
(Is. 41:21-24.)

The gods of the nations were merely idols, the work of man's
hands (Is. 44:9-20). There was only one God, Yahweh. If Israel
were to receive any help, that help would have to come from
Yahweh. The Second Isaiah was writing for a people which had
not only known defeat; it also had come to know despair.

This is the background for an explosion of exultant joy. The
Second Isaiah's theme was simple. We stand on the threshold of a
new exodus, a new act of divine mercy!

> 1) Comfort, comfort my people,
>   says your God.
> 2) Speak tenderly to Jerusalem,
>   and cry to her
>   that her warfare is ended,
>   that her iniquity is pardoned,
>   that she has received from the LORD's hand
>   double for all her sins.
>
> 3) A voice cries:
>   "In the wilderness prepare the way of
>   the LORD,
>   make straight in the desert a highway
>   for our God.
> 4) Every valley shall be lifted up,
>   and every mountain and hill be made low;
>   the uneven ground shall become level,
>   and the rough places a plain.
> 5) And the glory of the LORD shall be revealed,
>   and all flesh shall see it together,
>   for the mouth of the LORD has spoken."
>
> 6) A voice says, "Cry!"
>   And I said, "What shall I cry?"

All flesh is grass,
>   and all its beauty is like the flower
>   of the field.
7) The grass withers, the flower fades,
>   when the breath of the LORD blows upon it;
>   surely the people is grass.
8) The grass withers, the flower fades;
>   but the word of our God will stand for ever.

9) Get you up to a high mountain,
>   O herald of good tidings to Zion;
>   lift up your voice with strength,
>   O herald of good tidings to Jerusalem.[5]
>   Lift it up, fear not;
>   say to the cities of Judah,
>   "Behold your God!"
10) Behold, the Lord GOD comes with might,
>   and his arm rules for him;
>   behold, his reward is with him,
>   and his recompense before him.
11) He will feed his flock like a shepherd,
>   he will gather the lambs in his arms,
>   he will carry them in his bosom,
>   and gently lead those that are with young.
>   (Is. 40:1-11.)

Part of the Second Isaiah's greatness was his ability to see this in the turbulent events of his day. Part of his greatness was in the skill with which he transformed ancient themes and used them to convey his message. We might be able to enlarge our response to the Second Isaiah if we tried here to read him as he originally was read—by seeing his use of themes familiar to all his readers. There are too many of them to review here, but we can examine five.

Isaiah ben Amoz used the myth of the mountain of God as the framework for part of his message. This pictured God as defending a holy mountain and the people he had gathered there. As used in

137

the Old Testament, the mountain is often called Mount Zion. The myth told how the holy mountain would be attacked by enemies, but how their assaults would be crushed suddenly by God. This display of his power would be so clear a proof that he was the only God worthy of worship that Zion would be both a place of refuge for his people and also a place of pilgrimage for all the nations of earth.

Parts of the holy mountain theme appear scattered throughout Isaiah 40–55. Isaiah 42:13-16 pictures Yahweh as waging war, and Isaiah 44:26-28; 52:1-3; and 54:11-17 speak of the restoration of the holy city. Isaiah 52:8-9 equates Jerusalem with Zion. The highway of God in Isaiah 40:3-5 may reflect the sacred highway built in Babylonia for the processions in which idols of Babylon's gods were carried, but there are at least two mountain of God themes here also: a change in the landscape which makes the mountain of God more visible, and the spectacular quality of God's saving act. The motif of the nations coming to Zion to bring gifts and to give their allegiance appears in Isaiah 45:14-15 and 49:7, 22-23. The Second Isaiah does not use the whole myth as one of his disciples, the author of Isaiah 60, did.

The nearest the Second Isaiah came to using the complete myth of the mountain of God is in Isaiah 52:7-12.

> 7) How beautiful upon the mountains
>   are the feet of him who brings good tidings,
>   who publishes peace, who brings good tidings
>   of good,
>   who publishes salvation,
>   who says to Zion, "Your God reigns."
> 8) Hark, your watchmen lift up their voice,
>   together they sing for joy;
>   for eye to eye they see
>   the return of the LORD to Zion.
> 9) Break forth together into singing,
>   you waste places of Jerusalem;

for the LORD has comforted his people,
he has redeemed Jerusalem.
10) The LORD has bared his holy arm
before the eyes of all the nations;
and all the ends of the earth shall see
the salvation of our God.

11) Depart, depart, go out thence,
touch no unclean thing;
go out from the midst of her, purify
yourselves,
you who bear the vessels of the LORD.
12) For you shall not go out in haste,
and you shall not go in flight,
for the LORD will go before you,
and the God of Israel will be your rear guard.

The event being described is God's deliverance of his people. This act is carried out by making possible the escape from Babylonia, as verses 11 and 12 make clear. It is to be a deed so strange that all peoples will see in it a display of God's power (vs. 10). But even this passage lacks several parts of the theme. We can only conclude that the Second Isaiah did not believe that the myth of the mountain of God as a whole expressed his convictions well.

The second cultic tradition the Second Isaiah used is the creation myth which lies behind Genesis 1. The Babylonian form of the myth is called the Enuma Elish.[6] It tells how the high gods created chaos and begot a family of divine children, entrusting the rule of chaos to the oldest of these children. The other offspring became restless however, and one of them defeated the chaos deity and created the world by bringing order out of chaos.

If we remember that the Second Isaiah wrote at a time when many Israelites living in Babylonia were being attracted to Babylonian religion, verses scattered through Isaiah 40–55 suddenly become important. Many of these are echoes of some part of the Babylonian creation story—such as the statement that Yahweh, not the Babylonian god Marduk, stretched out the heavens.

Thus says God, the LORD,
who created the heavens and stretched
them out,
who spread forth the earth and what comes
from it,
who gives breath to the people upon it
and spirit to those who walk in it: . . .
(Is. 42:5; see also 40:21-22; 44:24; 45:12;
48:13; 51:13, 16.)

Two references are distinctive and important. The first is Isaiah
45:18-19.

18) For thus says the LORD,
who created the heavens
(he is God!),
who formed the earth and made it
(he established it;
he did not create it a chaos,
he formed it to be inhabited!):
"I am the LORD, and there is no other.
19) I did not speak in secret,
in a land of darkness;
I did not say to the offspring of Jacob,
'Seek me in chaos.'
I the LORD speak the truth,
I declare what is right."

The Babylonian myth told of creation in two stages: the
creation of formless matter and the gods, and the creation of our
world after the defeat of the chaos god. Notice how vigorously
the Second Isaiah disagreed with the Babylonian myth. Yahweh
alone is the creator. There never was a universe of formless matter.
From the beginning, this world was intended to be a home for
mankind. God's original plan was to create our world as it now is,
and it is the realm in which he discloses himself.

The second passage is Isaiah 51:9-11.

9) Awake, awake, put on strength,
    O arm of the LORD;
  awake, as in days of old,
    the generations of long ago.
  Was it not thou that didst cut Rahab in pieces,
    that didst pierce the dragon?
10) Was it not thou that didst dry up the sea,
    the waters of the great deep;
  that didst make the depths of the sea a way
    for the redeemed to pass over?
11) And the ransomed of the LORD shall return,
    and come with singing to Zion;
  everlasting joy shall be upon their heads;
    they shall obtain joy and gladness,
    and sorrow and sighing shall flee away.

We pick up a reference here to the conflict between the chaos god and the savior deity who created the world which is so precise that two of the Old Testament's names for the chaos deity are used, Rahab and the dragon. In Isaiah 45:18-19, the Second Isaiah denied that the myth told the story of creation correctly. Here he equated the myth with a historical event, the crossing of the Red Sea during the exodus. The reference to the crossing of the sea is then applied immediately to the forthcoming escape from the exile.

The freedom with which the Second Isaiah used elements in the ancient creation story suggests that he did not take it literally. But he did make use of the myth, and he was not a man to use words idly. Why did he link together part of the creation story, the exodus from Egypt, and the future deliverance from Babylonia?

A third theme to appear in the Second Isaiah is the garden of God myth. We cannot reconstruct this myth here in any detail. As we have already seen, the myth told of a garden of God in which the tree of life grew, tended by the royal gardener and watered by the waters of life welling up out of the abyss below. The waters of life then flowed out from the garden to bring life to all the world. The priest-king-gardener himself was sometimes said to be the tree of life, or one of its branches or roots.

Isaiah 41:17-20 is a reflection of the garden of God theme.

> 17) When the poor and needy seek water,
>   and there is none,
>   and their tongue is parched with thirst,
>   I the LORD will answer them,
>   I the God of Israel will not forsake them.
> 18) I will open rivers on the bare heights,
>   and fountains in the midst of the valleys;
>   I will make the wilderness a pool of water,
>   and the dry land springs of water.
> 19) I will put in the wilderness the cedar,
>   the acacia, the myrtle, and the olive;
>   I will set in the desert the cypress,
>   the plane and the pine together;
> 20) that men may see and know,
>   may consider and understand together,
>   that the hand of the LORD has done this,
>   the Holy One of Israel has created it.

The Second Isaiah is saying here that Yahweh will create for Israel a garden in which it can drink again the waters of life and live again in the shade of the tree of life. Is this also the significance of Isaiah 51:3? And are we to see behind the strange statement in chapter 53:2 the motif of the priest-king who is sometimes described in the myth as a root of the tree of life?

We already have enough evidence to support the claim that the Second Isaiah tended to state his message in terms of themes which had long histories and which aroused tremendous response. A study of the words and the titles of address he used would show that he picked his words with the same care that he selected his themes. It is not strange, therefore, that the fourth theme to be reviewed here is the tradition of the exodus from Egypt. The three themes

The Exilic Prophets

already reviewed were shared with other ancient peoples. The tradition of the exodus was unique to Israel.

There are two major references to the exodus in Isaiah 40–55. Both are odd. We have already examined one of them (Is. 51:9-11), a passage in which the exodus is equated with the savior god's defeat of the god of chaos as reported in the creation myth. Both exodus and creation are likened to the forthcoming escape from the Babylonian exile. The other passage is Isaiah 43:16-21.

16) Thus says the LORD,
      who makes a way in the sea,
      a path in the mighty waters,
17) who brings forth chariot and horse,
      army and warrior;
    they lie down, they cannot rise,
      they are extinguished, quenched like
      a wick:
18) "Remember not the former things,
      nor consider the things of old.
19) Behold, I am doing a new thing;
      now it springs forth, do you not perceive
      it?
    I will make a way in the wilderness
      and rivers in the desert.
20) The wild beasts will honor me,
      the jackals and the ostriches;
    for I give water in the wilderness,
      rivers in the desert,
    to give drink to my chosen people,
21)   the people whom I formed for myself
      that they might declare my praise."

If we remember that the ancient Israelites often equated the sea and the abyss of the creation myth, we will find in verses 16 and 17 the same meaning we discovered in Isaiah 51:9-11. The Second Isaiah again has equated the exodus of Israelite clans from Egypt

143

with the defeat of the chaos god in the creation myth. But verses 18 and 19 urge Israel to forget this splendid past because God is about to do something even more splendid. This is the deliverance of the Israelites from their enslavement to Babylonia. It is described by using the theme of the gift of the water of life taken from the garden of God myth. Thus in one passage the Second Isaiah said that the escape from Babylonia would be a new creation of Israel similar to the first creation during the exodus from Egypt. In the other passage, we are urged to forget the earlier divine act and look only for a new act in which God will give his people new life.

This disagreement suggests that the Second Isaiah is trying, in both passages, to say something about the return from exile, rather than about the exodus from Egypt. He used the tradition of the exodus just as he used the myths of the mountain of God, the creation story, and the garden of God—almost as a tool. He was trying to communicate to his contemporaries not only the statement, "God is about to save us again from slavery," but also his excitement, his certainty, his exultation, and his awe. He chose to do this by using four ancient, powerful traditions as similes for something new, something greater than any one of the ancient traditions alone. The God of their fathers had chosen once again to intervene to save the people he had punished. The Second Isaiah saw this as a more remarkable, more sovereign act than either the creation or the exodus.

When earlier prophets spoke of the exodus, they often put the matter in such a way that it is clear that they believed that it was the beginning of the history of their people. Israel had been created during the escape from Egypt. The earliest event in Israelite history mentioned by Amos is the exodus (Amos 2:10). Hosea called the period of slavery in Egypt the childhood of Israel (Hos. 11:1). Jeremiah pictured the wilderness wandering as the honeymoon in the marriage of Yahweh and Israel (Jer. 2:1). But when the Second Isaiah reached back to the origins of his people, it was to Abraham and Sarah.

1) Hearken to me, you who pursue deliverance,
      you who seek the LORD;
   look to the rock from which you were hewn,
      and to the quarry from which you were
         digged.
2) Look to Abraham your father
      and to Sarah who bore you;
   for when he was but one I called him,
      and I blessed him and made him many.

                              (Is. 51:1-2.)

This introduces us to the fifth theme in the Second Isaiah's message. It would be possible to say of Amos, Hosea, Jeremiah, and Ezekiel that they had a view of the history of their people with two chapters already written: the creation of the nation during the exodus and the faithlessness of the nation under the monarchy. Two chapters of their view of the history of their people remained to be written: the destruction of the faithless people and a new deliverance from slavery for the survivors of the destruction.

The Second Isaiah's view of his people's history differed from this at several points. Israel began with Abraham and Sarah. The exodus was an act of divine mercy as great as the victory of the savior god over the chaos god in the creation myth. The people whom Yahweh had created and had rescued from slavery had disobeyed his will and had been punished, but the covenant had not been broken. It was carved on the palms of God's hands (Is. 49:16). Only God could abrogate it, and he had not. The exile had been punishment, not abandonment.

> Thus says the LORD:
> "Where is your mother's bill of divorce,
>   with which I put her away?
> Or which of my creditors is it
>   to whom I have sold you?
> Behold, for your iniquities you were sold,

and for your transgressions your mother was
put away."

(Is. 50:1.)

God had retained his royal sovereignty over Israel throughout.
When the punishment has been completed, and Israel had been
restored, a new role for it would begin. This role is described in
those passages which speak of a servant of the Lord.

The "servant of the Lord" is the fifth theme in the prophet's
message. It appears in Isaiah 41:8-10; 42:1-9, 18-25; 43:8-10;
44:1-2, 21-22; 44:24-45:13; 48:20; 49:1-6; 50:10; 52:13-53:12.

These verses create problems so difficult that scholars have
debated them vigorously. Every major solution has been defended
by someone.[7] We are not excused by this from reaching a conclusion ourselves, but scholars have explored such a large number
of possibilities that we approach the problem knowing before we
start where certain basic choices will lead us.

The first choice is to decide whether or not all the references to
the servant are the work of the Second Isaiah. The servant is
identified as Israel in Isaiah 41:8; 44:1-2; 45:4; and 48:20. If the
Second Isaiah wrote all the passages mentioning the servant and
had the same identification for the servant in mind throughout, we
begin our study knowing that the servant is Israel.

If, however, we agree with those scholars who argue that the
Second Isaiah did not write certain passages (Is. 42:1-4; 49:1-6;
52:13-53:12), or that he wrote them at a time when he had a
servant other than Israel in mind, the fact that Israel is not
identified as the servant in these passages—except in 49:3, a
verse sometimes held to be a later addition—makes it possible to
claim that the servant in these verses could have been an individual.
Then the search for that individual begins. Some odd suggestions
have been made.

I believe that the Second Isaiah wrote all the servant passages,
and that he had the same servant in mind throughout. This means
that I believe that the servant is Israel. Now we face a second

146

group of decisions. The nature of our problem here is simple. The servant is supposed to redeem Israel (Is. 49:5-6; 53:4-12). If Israel is the servant, how can the servant redeem the servant? The choice that has to be made here is among the several ways in which it would be possible to speak of Israel as redeeming itself. It has been suggested that the contrast is between the real, historical Israel—which needed to be saved—and an ideal Israel; or that it is between all Israel—which needed redemption—and a small and faithful core in Israel. Since I find nowhere else in the Old Testament a contrast between a "real" anything and an "ideal" anything, I have chosen the second of these possibilities.

By this time, we have pressed the identification of the servant far enough to make it clear that the role of the servant—what it is to do, and how it is to act—is as important as the identification. All Israel was a subject people when the prophet wrote, and thus relatively helpless. If we identify the servant as a part of a helpless people, the part is more helpless than the whole. Clearly, whatever was to be done through Israel—either all Israel or a part of it—was to be done by someone acting upon it from the outside. Israel was to serve because that which was done to it would affect others. It was God who was to act, and his salvation of a helpless part of Israel was to be such a clear proof of his will and power that all would be drawn to Israel's God. Since the act foreseen by the Second Isaiah was the return by God of the exiles, the actual saving act would be done to only a part of Israel; but the return of the exiles would restore all Israel, both those returning and those who had never left Palestine.

> 1) Who has believed what we have heard?
>   And to whom has the arm of the LORD been
>   revealed?
> 2) For he grew up before him like a young plant,
>   and like a root out of dry ground;
>   he had no form or comeliness that we should
>   look at him,
>   and no beauty that we should desire him.

3) He was despised and rejected by men;
   a man of sorrows, and acquainted with
        grief;
   and as one from whom men hide their faces
      he was despised, and we esteemed him not.

4) Surely he has borne our griefs
   and carried our sorrows;
   yet we esteemed him stricken,
      smitten by God, and afflicted.
5) But he was wounded for our transgressions,
   he was bruised for our iniquities;
   upon him was the chastisement that made us
        whole,
   and with his stripes we are healed.
                          (Is. 53:1-5; but see
                          the entire chapter.)

God had created Israel, had guided it, had taught it, had punished it, and now was about to restore it in order that it might become, through its agony,

    6b) a covenant to the people,
        a light to the nations,
    7)   to open the eyes that are blind,
        to bring out the prisoners from the dungeon,
        from the prison those who sit in darkness.
                          (Is. 42:6b-7.)

Centuries later, an early Christian found in these words a description of the ministry of our Lord (Lk. 4:16-19). Once again, a prophet had found the word of God in suffering.

SUMMARY

The Christian study of the prophets has gone through several periods. The first was the study of the prophetic books to find in them predictions of the coming of Christ. The second was the discovery in the oracles of the prophets of the origins of the ethical and spiritual truths upon which Christianity is built. These truths were summed up in the term "ethical monotheism." [8]

When it was thought that the prophets had originated ethical monotheism, the question of the kind of genius that made it possible for them to discover this truth became important. The problem of the nature of genius is difficult. The question of the nature of religious genius is even more difficult. The examination of this concentrated on the nature of a prophet's self-awareness or the nature of the prophetic experience. [9]

The study of the prophetic experience swiftly became a study of the presence of abnormality in a prophet. The term most widely used was ecstasy. This was a poor choice because it has such a wide range of meanings, all the way from a form of madness to the creative inspiration of the artist. When attention had become fixed on the prophets' abnormalty, it became necessary to study their culture in order to determine whether or not they were abnormal in terms of their own culture. Since their culture was God-centered, it could hardly be studied without attention being given to the relationship of the prophet to the public worship of his age, both to the rites and institutions of worship and to the beliefs expressed therein. Thus the prophets came to be studied in terms of the traditions and practices of the cult in which they participated. This has been such a study.

Studying a prophet in this way does not mean that other ways are wrong or are without value. Although many of us today would doubt that the prophets consciously predicted the coming of Christ, it still remains true that Christ cannot be understood without knowing as much as possible about his forebears. It also is true that the more we know about those forebears the clearer it becomes that Christ does fulfill them. It is not an idle pastime to look back into the prophets of the Old Testament in order to understand the ministry of our Lord. One needs only to ponder the figure of the servant of the Lord as described by the Second Isaiah to find the servant made real in the life and passion of Christ. If we have any criticism of earlier generations of Christians in their use of the prophets of the Old Testament, it is that they were too mechanical and too superficial. They sought evidence of fulfillment so eagerly that they failed to reach a profound understanding of the prophets.

We also need to continue the kind of study of the prophets that seeks to find in them the origins of our most basic modern beliefs. The roots for most of our ethical ideals are to be found in the words of the prophets of the Old Testament, even though the prophets did not intend to establish a moral philosophy. The life of ancient Israel and ancient Greece are the sources of modern civilization, even though the sources differ radically from what has developed from them.

But both types of study of the prophets are inquiries into the past in which we ask former ages questions we want answered. This is always proper and often necessary. The ancient Romans had no science of economics, but insofar as economic history is important to economics, a reconstruction by a modern historian of the economy of the ancient Roman Epire is important. [10] We are Christians; the prophets were not. We ask about the relationship between the prophets and Christ. We build philosophical and ethical systems; the prophets did not. We ask about the prophets' contributions to our system of ideas.

There is another approach to history, however. This is the attempt to reconstruct as much of the world of the mind of the past as possible in order to enter into that world and listen. When we do this, we attempt to understand the problems our forefathers faced in order to hear them speak about those problems. We do not turn to the past for solutions to modern problems. We turn to the past for renewal. Man is a historical being. He lives as long as his past lives in him. He dies as a man when his past dies. It is essential for our existence to stand where our forefathers stood and to hear them speak. The past is where our roots lie; and just as no tree is stronger than its roots, so no man is more vital than his roots.

HISTORICAL CHART [11]

Date	Israelite Rulers		Events	Prophet
	in Judah	*in Israel*		
786		Jeroboam II (786-746)	Israel most powerful kingdom in the area	
783	Uzziah (783-742)			Amos (c. 760)
746		Zechariah (746-745)		Hosea (745?-735?)
745		Shallum (745)	came to throne by revolt	
745		Menahem (745-738)	came to throne by revolt; paid tribute to Assyria	
742	Jotham* (750-735)			Isaiah (742-700?)
738		Pekahiah (738-737)		
737		Pekah (737-732)	came to throne by revolt	
735	Ahaz (735-715)			
734			attack on Judah by Israel and Syria. Assyria helps Judah and crushes Syria and Israel. Judah accepts Assyrian religion	
732		Hoshea (732-724)	came to throne by revolt	
724			Hoshea refused to pay Assyrian tribute. Assyria invaded Israel, Hoshea killed,	

* Uzziah was gravely ill during the closing years of his reign and shared the throne with Jotham.

Date	Israelite Rulers		Events	Prophet
	in Judah	*in Israel*		
722-721			Samaria besieged. Samaria falls. End of the northern kingdom	
715	Hezekiah (715-687)			
701			Hezekiah joins alliance against Assyria, is crushed but not deposed	
687	Manasseh (687-642)		Pro-Assyrian policy resumed. Yahwism persecuted	
671-667			Assyria conquers Egypt	
642	Amon (642-640)			
640	Josiah (640-609)			
625			Assyrian Empire crumbling. Babylonia frees itself	Jeremiah (626-586)
621			Josiah declares Judah independent. Deuteronomic Reformation	
614-609			Assyria destroyed by Babylonia. Egyptian attempt to help Assyria failed	
609			Josiah killed in battle trying to prevent Egypt from moving north to help Assyria	

Date	Israelite Rulers		Events	Prophet
	in Judah	*in Israel*		
609	Jehoiahaz (609)		Defeated Egyptians depose Jehoiahaz	
609	Jehoiakim (609-598)		Enthroned by Egyptians. Switched to Babylonians, then reverted to Egyptians. Besieged in Jerusalem by Babylonians. Died during the siege	
598	Jehoiachin (598-597)		Came to throne during the siege and surrendered. Taken to Babylon as captive	Ezekiel (598-580?)
597	Zedekiah (597-587)		Enthroned by Babylonians	
587			Zedekiah revolted Jerusalem captured and destroyed	
586-538			The Babylonian Exile	
540				The Second Isaiah (540-538)
538			Persia conquered Babylonia. Jews allowed to return to Palestine	

I Will Be Your God

NOTES

1. For detailed commentaries on the book of Ezekiel, see G. A. Cooke, *A Critical and Exegetical Commentary on the Book of Ezekiel* (New York: Charles Scribner's Sons, 1937); I. G. Matthews, *Ezekiel* (Philadelphia: American Baptist Publication Society, 1939); H. G. May, "Ezekiel: Introduction and Exegesis," *The Interpreter's Bible*, VI, 41-338. For briefer commentaries, see A. B. Davidson, *The Book of the Prophet Ezekiel, with Notes and Introduction* ("The Cambridge Bible for Schools and Colleges" [Cambridge: Cambridge University Press, 1893, 1906]); C. G. Howie, *The Book of Ezekiel, The Book of Daniel* ("The Layman's Bible Commentary" [Richmond: John Knox Press, 1961]).

2. So argued by Jack Finegan, "The Chronology of Ezekiel," *Journal of Biblical Literature*, LXIX (1950), 61-66, and in his *Handbook of Biblical Chronology* (Princeton: Princeton University Press, 1964), pp. 210-12.

3. See George Widengren, *The King and the Tree of Life in Ancient Near Eastern Religion* (Uppsala and Leipzig: A.-B. Lundequistska Bokhandeln, 1951).

4. Four recent commentaries on the Second Isaiah are available: James Muilenburg, "Isaiah, Chapters 40-66; Introduction and Exegesis," *The Interpreter's Bible*, V, 381-652; C. R. North, *The Second Isaiah; Introduction, Translation and Commentary to Chapters XL-LV* (Oxford: The Clarendon Press, 1964); G. A. F. Knight, *Deutero-Isaiah, a Theological Commentary on Isaiah 40-55* (Nashville: Abingdon Press, 1965); J. D. Smart, *History and Theology in Second Isaiah, a Commentary on Isaiah 35, 40-66* (Philadelphia: The Westminster Press, 1965). The authors of the following two commentaries argue for a very late date for Isaiah 40-66: C. C. Torrey, *The Second Isaiah: A New Interpretation* (New York: Charles Scribner's Sons, 1928); and U. E. Simon, *A Theology of Salvation: A Commentary on Isaiah 40-55* (New York: The Macmillan Company, 1953). J. Skinner, *The Book of the Prophet Isaiah, with Introduction and Notes* ("Cambridge Bible for Schools and Colleges" [Cambridge: Cambridge University Press, 1897, 1951]), is an older, shorter commentary. See also note 7 for chapter 4 for commentaries on the whole of the book of Isaiah.

5. A comparison of this with the Revised Standard Version will give the two translations of the Hebrew text possible here. Either is grammatically possible. The alternate translation used here seems to me to fit better both the poetic parallelism and the cultic traditions lying behind the passage.

6. Available in an English translation by E. A. Speiser in Pritchard, ed., *Ancient Near Eastern Texts*, pp. 60-72 and *The Ancient Near East, an Anthology*, pp. 31-39.

154

7. C. R. North, *The Suffering Servant in Deutero-Isaiah; an Historical and Critical Study* (London: Oxford University Press, 1948), contains an excellent survey of the debate and defends a different conclusion from the one reached here.
8. As exemplified by J. M. P. Smith, *The Prophets and Their Times.*
9. As exemplified by J. Lindblom, *Prophecy in Ancient Israel.* For a review of this debate, see H. H. Rowley, "The Nature of Prophecy in Recent Study," *Harvard Theological Review,* XXXVIII (1945), 1-38.
10. This has been done. See Tenney Frank, ed., *An Economic Survey of Ancient Rome* (6 vols., Baltimore: The Johns Hopkins Press, 1936-1959).
11. The dates for the reigns of the Israelite kings in the chart are taken from *The Westminster Historical Atlas to the Bible.* Rev. and ed. by George Edward Wright and Floyd V. Filson. Copyright 1956 by W. L. Jenkins. The Westminster Press. Used by permission.

VI

THE PSALMS

The Psalms of the Old Testament have always been used by Christians in public and private worship. Even those who claim no knowledge of the Old Testament will know the 23rd psalm, and they find that many others are familiar when they read through the book of Psalms.

This creates a problem. Several times the text of the psalms used in public worship has remained the text of an older and familiar translation when major new translations of the Bible have appeared. In AD. 383 Jerome revised an older Latin translation of the Psalms, and this is still used in the services in St. Peter's in Rome, rather than the Vulgate which Jerome translated directly from the Hebrew text of the Old Testament a few years later. Centuries later, the Anglican *Book of Common Prayer* continued to use the text of the Psalms from the Great Bible of 1539, even though the King James Version of 1611 had come into general use. The 1964 edition of the Ritual of The Methodist Church has retained the King James Version for the translation of 23rd psalm in its funeral service, even though all the other scriptural readings proposed for that service are printed according to the Revised Standard Version.[1]

The Psalms have become so intimate a part of our faith that we resist any change in our understanding of them. Part of their greatness, however, lies in the many ways they can be used and understood. We need therefore to recognize that all great religious literature has at least two levels of meaning: the original meaning and the meaning for us. One of the reasons we try to recover the original meaning is to enrich the meaning for us. It is hoped that such will be the result of this chapter.

We begin by noting that several psalms appear twice.[2] Psalm

14 differs from psalm 53 in using Lord (Yahweh) rather than God (Elohim). Psalms 42 to 83 use God (Elohim) far more often than Lord (Yahweh). Parts of psalms 57 and 60 reappear as psalm 108. Psalm 72:20 closes, "The prayers of David, the son of Jesse, are ended." Psalm 73 is "A Psalm of Asaph," and if we group the psalms according to personal names used in their titles, we find that psalms 50, 73-83 are assigned to Asaph, and psalms 42, 44-49, 84, 85, 87, and 88 are assigned to the "Sons of Korah." This is enough evidence to make one wonder if the book of Psalms might not be a group of older collections of psalms.

It was assumed for many centuries that David was the author of the book of Psalms because his name appears so often in the titles. Because of this, many thought of the Psalms as a collection of religious poems written by David. The suggestion that it is a merger of several once independent collections, two of which were called "Psalms of the Sons of Korah" and "Psalms of Asaph," carries with it a different conclusion.

According to 2 Chronicles 20:19, the Sons of Korah were a guild of Temple singers, and Asaph is described in 1 Chronicles 15:17 as one of the three leaders of the choir of the Levites in the Temple. If these are reliable traditions, two of the collections making up the book of Psalms were gathered by professional Temple singers. This suggests that the psalms were once parts of the Temple liturgy, for it was the duty of the Temple singers to chant the liturgy.

A review of the use of personal names in the titles of psalms gives interesting results. The titles fall into seven classes: There are fifty-one psalms lacking a personal name in their titles, seventy-two psalms using David, eleven psalms using Korah, twelve psalms using Asaph, two psalms using Solomon, one psalm using Ethan the Ezrahite, and one psalm using Moses. Fifty-five psalms have titles which are instructions to the choirmaster. He presumably was the director of the professional singers who chanted the Temple liturgy, all of whom are said to have been Levites. This makes one suspect that the titles, "A Psalm of David," "A Psalm of

Asaph," or "A Psalm of Korah," may really have been suggestions
to the choir describing the kind of music or chanting to be used.
It also strengthens the deduction that a large number of psalms
were originally part of the liturgy of the cult.

Many psalms preserve references to their use in the liturgy. If
we confine ourselves only to those verses which speak of practices
we would recognize at once as liturgical, we would have to list the
use of instrumental music and singing (Ps. 33:2-3), singing and
clapping the hands (Ps. 47:1, 6-7), summons to praise (Ps. 48:1),
ritual processions (Ps. 68:24-27), singing accompanied by instru-
ments (Ps. 98:4-6), dancing while singing (Ps. 149:2-3, 5-6),
and dancing accompanied by music (Ps. 150:3-5).

The evidence is convincing. Even though we do not yet
fully understand the significance of all the psalm titles, and even
though the liturgy and personnel of the ancient Jerusalem Temple
are not fully known to us, we can say with confidence that many
of the psalms originally were parts of a liturgy. This does not
mean that they are rightly used only when they are sung by a
congregation—as many of them still are—but it does mean that we
may be able to enrich our appreciation of them by seeing them
again in their cultic context.

Before we can do this, two other matters need to be mentioned.
Many Protestants dislike the phrase, "the liturgy of the cult."
There may be important historical reasons for this, but we should
not be led into misunderstanding by them. The word "cult" means
here the accepted or normal form of public worship. The prayer
meetings many of us have attended are a part of the Protestant
cult. They have a fixed form. They open with several gospel
hymns, often chosen by the congregation. A scripture lesson is
read, explained, and applied to our lives. Other hymns may follow,
and then the congregation prays together. This part of the service
opens with prayers by laymen. Some of these are stereotyped, some
wander, others are hurried, inarticulate but urgent. Major personal
crises are often shared. There are two accepted ways of ending
the period of prayer. The leader, usually the pastor, may close with

a prayer for all the congregation, followed by a closing hymn and benediction; or he may start singing a hymn softly. Many of us who have known the prayer meeting think of it as the essence of free worship, yet it is as much a cultic act as the Mass of the Roman Catholic Church. It is an accepted, normal form of public worship.

The word "liturgy," of course, is the term for the words said or sung regularly in public worship. The prayer books used by Roman Catholics, Lutherans, and Episcopalians contain their liturgies, but the gospel songs and the Bible contain much of the liturgy used in prayer meetings. The rest was oral tradition.

When we say, "the liturgy of the cult," we mean the elements which can be, and often are, used in the normal service of public worship. All the hymns a congregation sings are part of its liturgy, even though there is choice among the hymns available. All congregations have a liturgy. All congregations participate in a cult. We differ among ourselves in the flexibility and the variety permitted by our practice.

The final preliminary matter we should mention is a question which has not been solved. Do the liturgical psalms reflect one great festival extending through the year,[3] or several independent festivals? If we were to state the question in modern terms, we would ask: Do all our hymns reflect a single festival of which Christmas and Easter are parts, or do the Christmas and Easter hymns reflect two Christian festivals? If all that we knew about our cult was what we could deduce from our hymns, could we answer this? The editors of our hymnals assume that we know about our own festivals. They do not identify and explain them for us. The editors of the book of Psalms assumed a similar knowledge of ancient Jewish worship which we lack. All that we have are hints preserved here and there.

As a result scholars do not fully agree on the reconstruction of the Jewish liturgical calendar. The view given here is that the Israelite cult included several major festivals which had different histories and beliefs. At least two of the festivals were Canaanite in origin. One was Israelite. They came eventually to be related to one another, but we will speak of them as separate. The festivals, or liturgies, about which we will speak are the coronation ceremony, the enthronement festival, the covenant renewal festival, and liturgies of petition.

THE CORONATION CEREMONY

Psalm 45 is proof that there once were liturgies dealing with events in the life of the king. The psalmist began,

> My heart overflows with a goodly theme;
>   I address my verses to the king;
>   my tongue is like the pen of a ready scribe.
>   (Vs. 1.)

He then praised the king so boldly that he created a theological problem for later generations, as a glance at the various translations of verse 6 will show. Verses 10-15 address a royal bride.

> 10) Hear, O daughter, consider, and incline
>   your ear;
>   forget your people and your father's house;
> 11)   and the king will desire your beauty.
>   Since he is your lord, bow to him.

This psalm is part of a royal wedding ceremony.

The chief royal liturgy to have survived, however, is the coronation ceremony. 1 Kings 1:33-40 describes the coronation of Solomon; and 2 Kings 11:11-14 reports the crowning of Joash. We can fill in the accounts given us here by information surviving about similar Egyptian customs.[4] The coronation seems to have gone as follows. The candidate for the throne was taken to a shrine. This was the spring Gihon for Solomon and the Temple in Jerusalem for Joash. There they were anointed, crowned, and given the testimony. Egyptian parallels make it clear that the testimony, or the decree, was a document which gave the king his throne-name, empowered him to rule by the authority of God, and promised him divine support. The ceremony then shifted to the palace, where the king stood in a place dictated by tradition to read the testimony to the assembled court. He then was greeted with wildly joyful acclamation (1 Kings 1:40-45; 2 Kings 11:12). It is surprising how much of this can be found in the Psalms.

Psalm 72 begins:

> 1) Give the king thy justice, O God,
>   and thy righteousness to the royal son!
> 2) May he judge thy people with righteousness,
>   and thy poor with justice!
> 3) Let the mountains bear prosperity for the
>   people,
>   and the hills, in righteousness!
> 4) May he defend the cause of the poor of the
>   people,
>   give deliverance to the needy,
>   and crush the oppressor!

Then follows a petition for long life and victory (vss. 5-11), praise of the king's justice—described before he begins to rule apparently in order to try to influence him (vss. 12-14)—and further petitions for long life for the king and prosperity during his reign (vss. 15-17). The psalm closes with praise for Yahweh (vss. 18-19).

If we remember that the second half of a line often repeats the first half in Hebrew poetry, we can see that the entire psalm is a petition to God about the forthcoming reign of a king called "the royal son." It is probable, therefore, that this psalm was part of the liturgy sung as the prince was being brought into the sanctuary for the coronation. He is being presented to Yahweh, the God of Israel, with petitions describing the kind of reign his future subjects are hoping he will have.

Psalm 110 is a part of a liturgy in which God speaks directly to the king, inviting him to sit on his right hand and promising him victory.

1) The LORD says to my lord:
   "Sit at my right hand,
   till I make your enemies
   your footstool."
2) The LORD sends forth from Zion
   your mighty scepter.
   Rule in the midst of your foes!

This psalm also describes the king as a priest.

> The LORD has sworn
> and will not change his mind,
> "You are a priest for ever
> after the order of Melchizedek."
> (Vs. 4.)

It is reasonable to expect the coronation liturgy to state at some point that Yahweh had accepted the new king and would support his rule. This is what the document handed the king during the coronation asserted, and psalm 110 may have been chanted at precisely the point in the service when the king was given the testimony.

Psalm 2 quotes the testimony.

7) I will tell of the decree of the LORD:
   He said to me, "You are my son,
   today have I begotten you.
8) Ask of me, and I will make the nations your
   heritage,
   and the ends of the earth your possession.
9) You shall break them with a rod of iron,
   and dash them in pieces like a potter's vessel."

Our reconstruction of the coronation pictured the king as standing in a place in the court dictated by tradition and reading the text of the decree, or testimony, to the people. In this example, God tells the king that he is God's adopted son who has been given a son's access to his father's favor and power. Therefore God promises the king victory over his enemies.

Psalm 21 also seems to be part of a royal festival. It opens with a priest praising God on behalf of the king for God's faithfulness to the king (vss. 1-7), and it closes with a reply from God—perhaps given by a prophet attached to the Temple—assuring the king that God's support will continue (vss. 8-12). Psalm 20 may be the priestly benediction which ended the coronation ceremony. Psalm 89 recalls the coronation. Verses 19-37 report God's promises to the Davidic dynasty, and this passage is a detailed statement of the content of the testimony. Verses 38-51, however, make it clear that this psalm is not part of the coronation liturgy.

> 38) But now thou hast cast off and rejected,
>   thou art full of wrath against thy
>   anointed.
> 39) Thou hast renounced the covenant with thy
>   servant;
>   thou hast defiled his crown in the dust. . . .
> 46) How long, O LORD? Wilt thou hide thyself
>   for ever?
>   How long will thy wrath burn like fire?

By the time this psalm was composed, the monarchy had ended. The coronation ceremony was no longer being observed. This psalm comes from the exile, or later, and is a petition to God asking him to restore the Davidic dynasty and to renew his covenant with the king.[5]

This review of the liturgy of the coronation raises some odd problems. The royal decree reported in psalm 2:7-9 was fiercely nationalistic and mentioned only the military support God would give, but the petition for a decree chanted as the prince was presented for coronation (Ps. 72:1-4) asked also that the king be given the wisdom to rule justly and mercifully. Does this reflect a tension within the Jerusalem cult in which spokesmen for the court wanted divine support only for the king's authority, but spokesmen for the people wanted divine help in getting a just king? This is not impossible. Such a tension faces us today. Those of us who believe that government, whatever its form, derives its authority to rule ultimately from God have both the right and the duty to ask whether the authority being exercised in government is for its own benefit or for the welfare of the whole people of God. We Christians might be far more relevant today—a polite way of saying far more troublesome—if we celebrated the divine empowerment of our elected representatives and officials. We at least would constantly be reminded of the nature of divine authority to govern.

THE ENTHRONEMENT FESTIVAL

The coronation ceremony should not be confused with the enthronement festival. The former marked the crowning of the earthly king at the beginning of his reign; the latter celebrated the ascent of the god to the throne from which he ruled the world.

The enthronement festival was the liturgical reenactment of the creation myth. The yearly rise and fall of fertility was explained as a result of an annual revival of the battle between the savior god and the chaos deity in the beginning, after which the victorious savior god had formed the world out of the formless stuff which the chaos deity had ruled.

Each year as the earth turned brown and seemed to die, the chaos deity was believed again temporarily to have got the upper hand. One of the Canaanite mythology tablets describes how El, the father of all the gods, received the news that the savior god, Baal had been killed. The messengers report:

> We came upon Baal
>   Fallen on the ground:
> Puissant Baal is dead,
>   The Prince, Lord of Earth, is perished.
> Straightway Kindly El Benign

Descends from the throne,
Sits on the footstool;
From the footstool,
And sits on the ground;
Pours dust of mourning on his head,
Earth of mortification on his pate;
And puts on *sackcloth and loincloth.*
He *cuts a gash* with a stone,
Incisions with . . .
He gashes his cheeks and his chin.[6]

El's lamentation and self-mutilation recalls Hosea 7:14:

They do not cry to me from the heart,
but they wail upon their beds;
for grain and wine they gash themselves,
they rebel against me.

Eventually Baal escapes from the power of Mot, the chaos deity, and another tablet reports:

And behold, alive is [Puissant Baal]!
And behold, existent the Prince,
Lo[rd of Earth]!
In a dream, O kindly El Benign,
In a vision, Creator of Creatures,
The heavens fat did rain,
The wadies flow with honey.
So I knew
That alive was Puissant Baal!
Existent the Prince, Lord of Earth![7]

Baal then returns, mounts his throne again, and resumes his rule.

Unlike the coronation ceremony with which a king began his rule, the enthronement festival was repeated each year. Ancient man knew that he was part of the world in which he lived and believed that he had to parallel in his worship the basic rhythms of that world. We suspect today that he believed that those rhythms would cease should part of creation not act them out each year. The ritual enactment in the shrine of the revival of the savior god was needed if fertility were to return. The rite was basic to survival and was carried out earnestly and faithfully.

We have only parts of the liturgy of the enthronement festival in the Old Testament. The liturgy seems to have included these elements: (1) the search for and the discovery of the missing savior God, (2) the ritual procession to his palace or the shrine, (3) his ascent of his throne, and (4) the acclamation of the savior god as the divine king.[8]

The ritual procession to the shrine after the missing god had been found included a liturgy of entrance. As the procession arrived at the gateway, the gatekeepers of the house of the Lord and the people in the procession debated the right of entry.

> 3) Who shall ascend the hill of the LORD?
>   and who shall stand in his holy place?
> 4) He who has clean hands and a pure heart,
>   who does not lift up his soul to what is
>   false,
>   and does not swear deceitfully.
> (Ps. 24:3-4).

Then members of the procession and the gatekeepers chanted:

> 7) Lift up your heads, O gates!
>   and be lifted up, O ancient doors!
>   that the King of glory may come in.
> 8) Who is the King of glory?
>   The LORD, strong and mighty,
>   the LORD, mighty in battle!
> 9) Lift up your heads, O gates!
>   and be lifted up, O ancient doors!
>   that the King of glory may come in.
> 10) Who is this King of glory?

> The LORD of hosts,
> he is the King of glory!
> (Ps. 24:7-10.)

Yahweh Sabaoth, translated here as "the LORD of hosts," was the ancient Israelite name for its God, and the magnificent chant of entry ended with the shout, "Yahweh Sabaoth is the King of glory!"

This is fitting prelude to the coronation reflected in psalm 47. According to form critics, this is a hymn and opens with a call to praise.

> Clap your hands, all peoples!
> Shout to God [Elohim] with loud songs
> of joy!
> (Ps. 47:1.)

The hymn form then asks for what reason the worshipers are called to praise, and verses 2-4 review the greatness and the royal deeds of Yahweh.

> 2) For the LORD, the Most High, is terrible,
> a great king over all the earth.
> 3) He subdued peoples under us,
> and nations under our feet.
> 4) He chose our heritage for us,
> the pride of Jacob whom he loves.

The ancient Israelite was firmly convinced that the greatness of a deity was reflected in the greatness of his deeds. Yahweh was great because he had made a tiny people so strong that it ruled its neighbors.

Thus far the psalm has asked all nations to praise Elohim. It has then explained that all should praise Yahweh because he is a great king. Now, in verse 5, Yahweh mounts his throne and becomes Elohim.

> God has gone up with a shout,
> the LORD with the sound of a trumpet.

The psalm breaks immediately into acclamation, praising the reenthroned king for his greatness (vss. 6-10), and Israel's own name for the divine King, Yahweh, is not used again. Yahweh is Elohim, the God of all!

> 6) Sing praises to God, sing praises!
>   Sing praises to our King, sing praises!
> 7) For God is the king of all the earth;
>   sing praises with a psalm!

The longest part of the enthronement festival liturgy may have been the acclamation. More psalms reflect this part of the liturgy than any other. These psalms praise the greatness of Yahweh and describe his mighty deeds, often in terms of themes drawn from the creation myth. Psalms which seem to have belonged here in the festival include psalms 29, 93, 96, and 97. Psalm 29 asks the residents of heaven to join in the praise:

> Ascribe to the LORD, O heavenly beings,
> ascribe to the LORD glory and strength.
> (Vs. 1.)

It then describes the outpouring of Yahweh's might in nature (vss. 4-9). If you remember that the flood is one of the Old Testament terms for the abyss, the pre-creation chaos, you see how both the enthronement and the creation myth are reflected in a single verse.

> The LORD sits enthroned over the flood;
> The LORD sits enthroned as king for ever.
> (Vs. 10.)

Psalm 93 belongs in the liturgy after the ascent to the throne. It begins:

The LORD reigns; he is robed in majesty;
   the LORD is robed, he is girded with strength.

(Vs. 1.)

This psalm also echoes the theme of creation by describing Yahweh's royal power as greater than the power of chaos.

> 3) The floods have lifted up, O LORD,
>   the floods have lifted up their voice,
>   the floods lift up their roaring.
> 4) Mightier than the thunder of many waters,
>   mightier than the waves of the sea,
>   the LORD on high is mighty!

When we first meet this interpretation of many of the psalms, we tend to reject it. The ancient creation myth is just a curiosity for us, and we turn to modern science for truer descriptions of creation. The picture of God given here—a jealous divine king fighting constantly to maintain and to increase his authority— offends many of us. But we would be wise if we gave this ancient rite a second thought.

There are many elements both in the myth and in the reconstruction of the enthronement festival based on the myth which strike us as inadequate. Two thousand years in the future, men will find most of our best scientific beliefs equally inadequate. But have we come to the point where we deny that creation is bringing order out of chaos? This is one of the basic statements of the myth. A second affirmation is the belief that all people want to help to preserve order and to prevent a return to chaos. Is this undesirable? And precisely why do we recoil from the description of God as fighting to preserve the universe he has created?

Is it naïve of us to assume that we do not need such a festival?

THE COVENANT RENEWAL FESTIVAL

This is the Shechemite festival which has already been discussed in earlier chapters. The liturgy for this would recite the act by which Yahweh proved himself to be the divine King of the Israelite tribes—the guidance he gave during the exodus, wilderness wanderings, and invasion—and would renew the royal covenant based on that act. In that covenant, God promised to rule Israel if Israel would be faithful to him. The liturgy would report this also. The festival seems to have included curses and blessings, both of which appear in Deuteronomy 27 and 28. Are there any psalms which seem to reflect this liturgy?

Psalm 105 opens:

> 1) O give thanks to the LORD, call on his name,
> make known his deeds among the peoples!
> 2) Sing to him, sing praises to him,
> tell of all his wonderful works!

This is little more than a typical hymn introduction, but when the reason we are to praise is given, we have a recitation of the ancient saving history (vss. 5-44). There is no hint of the creation myth. The psalm then closes:

> to the end that they should keep his
> statutes,
> and observe his laws.
> Praise the LORD!
>
> (Vs. 45.)

This psalm reflects the basic structure of the covenant renewal festival. The deity is named. His display of royal power in history is described, and the obedience Israel should give him is stated. Psalm 114 is a briefer, more imaginative statement of the same themes, although it lacks the demand for obedience with which psalm 105 ends.

Two psalms recite the saving history—again with no reference to the creation myth—in order to warn Israel of the results of faithlessness. The first of these, psalm 81, also tells the saving history imaginatively.

5b) I hear a voice I had not known:
  6) "I relieved your shoulder of the burden;
      your hands were freed from the basket.
  7) In distress you called, and I delivered you;
      I answered you in the secret place of thunder;
      I tested you at the waters of Meribah.
  8) Hear, O my people, while I admonish you!
      O Israel, if you would but listen to me!
  9) There shall be no strange god among you;
      you shall not bow down to a foreign god.
 10) I am the Lord your God,
      who brought you up out of the land of Egypt.
      Open your mouth, and I will fill it."

The second, psalm 106, reminds us of the way Ezekiel told the saving history:

  6) Both we and our fathers have sinned;
      we have committed iniquity, we have done
        wickedly.
  7) Our fathers, when they were in Egypt,
      did not consider thy wonderful works;
      they did not remember the abundance of thy
        steadfast love,
      but rebelled against the Most High at
        the Red Sea.
  8) Yet he saved them for his name's sake,
      that he might make known his mighty power.

One gets the feeling that psalm 81 may have been preexilic and psalm 106 exilic or postexilic. Both stress Israel's faithlessness, but the former pictures God as willing still to restore Israel if Israel will repent. Psalm 106 is a confession of sin which closes with a plea for deliverance from exile:

    Save us, O Lord our God,
      and gather us from among the nations,

that we may give thanks to thy holy name
and glory in thy praise.
(Vs. 47.)

The covenant renewal festival, of course, would contain hymns
appropriate for victory and prosperity, as well as for temporary or
prolonged national disaster. These two psalms seem to have been
intended for use in hard times. Psalm 44 also reflects disaster but
differs from psalm 106 in the note of impatience it contains.

Rouse thyself! Why sleepest thou, O LORD?
Awake! Do not cast us off for ever!
(Vs. 23.)

Psalm 78 reflects ancient Israelite history in a puzzling way.
It also recites the history of salvation as if it were the history of
Israelite faithlessness, but it does this in order to assert that the
southern kingdom, Judah, and the kings of Judah ruling in Zion
—not the northern kingdom, Ephraim—was the only people
chosen by God.

67) He rejected the tent of Joseph,
he did not choose the tribe of Ephraim;
68) but he chose the tribe of Judah,
Mount Zion, which he loves.
69) He built his sanctuary like the high heavens,
like the earth, which he has founded for
ever.
70) He chose David his servant,
and took him from the sheepfolds;
71) from tending the ewes that had young he brought
him
to be the shepherd of Jacob his people,
of Israel his inheritance.

The problem this psalm creates for us is a historical one. Why was
it necessary so explicitly to read Ephraim out of Yahweh's favor?

Could it be because the exodus tradition had been at first the sacred tradition of the northern tribes only, but eventually became so important that the southern dynasty sought to claim it as its own?

None of the psalms attached here to the liturgy of the covenant renewal festival contains a reference to the creation myth mentioned in the enthronement festival psalms. This is enough reason to suspect that the two festivals originally were separate. The covenant renewal festival is associated with Shechem, as we saw in an earlier chapter. Because the enthronement festival in neighboring lands was celebrated by the royal court, it may have been the festival used in Jerusalem. If this were the case, the two festivals were celebrated in different places. One psalm, however, does merge the two liturgies. It has survived in the form of a chant sung by priest and congregation. Presumably the priest chanted the first line of each verse, and the congregation responded with the second line. Verses 4 to 9 recite the creation myth:

> 5) to him who by understanding made the heavens,
>   for his steadfast love endures for ever;
> 6) to him who spread out the earth upon the waters,
>   for his steadfast love endures for ever.
> (Ps. 136:5-6.)

Verses 10-22 then tell the ancient saving history of the Shechemite covenant renewal festival. There are some hints that the psalm may be late; but whether early or late, it indicates that the two once separate festivals were merged at some point in the history of the worship of ancient Israel.

We will return to the meaning of history for our faith in the closing chapter, and conclusions reached there will apply directly to this festival. The Hebrew-Christian tradition shares much of its content with the other religions in the midst of which it came into being. It is unique in its claim that God disclosed himself in specific events in history. This is the significance of our celebration both of Christmas and Easter. In terms of the history of public worship, the liturgy of the covenant renewal festival is the beginning of our worship of God's revelation of himself in time. When we abandon historical faith in our worship, we have ceased to be Christian.

LITURGIES OF PETITION

There is a large group of psalms which form critics call laments. Some may have been used by the king or the congregation on behalf of the nation, such as psalm 44. Others seem to have been part of a liturgy of petition used by individuals in distress. Only the laments themselves have come down to us. The liturgy in which they were used has been lost. Nevertheless, it is possible to reconstruct something of what was done and hoped for from the psalms themselves.[9]

The basic structure of the lament is as follows. The petitioner requests divine aid, explains why he needs it, and tries to persuade God to act on his behalf. His tone then changes to rejoicing just as if he had become convinced that his prayer had been heard and granted. The psalmist's explanation of why he needs divine aid tends to be given in very general terms because these psalms were used over and over again by different individuals. Many of the laments shift back and forth between these themes in a confusing way, but this very confusion suggests an intense feeling of distress.

Psalm 22 is an excellent example. It opens with words familiar to anyone who has attended a Good Friday service:

> My God, my God, why hast thou forsaken me?
> Why art thou so far from helping me, from
> the words of my groaning?
>
> (Vs. 1.)

Words of praise reflecting the sufferer's belief that God can help follow (vss. 3-5). With verse 6, a stylized description of suffering begins which extends through verse 18. Verses 19-21 repeat the request for aid, and the psalmist then bursts into a hymn of praise so abruptly that it was long thought that verses 22-31 must have been originally another psalm.

Other examples of liturgies of petition are psalms 7, 10, 12, 13, 17, 28, 31, and 38. Psalms 44, 60, 74, 80, 83, and 89 are group laments.[10]

SUMMARY

The understanding of the psalms that is proposed here asks us to read them as if they were liturgies for a group's worship rather than poetic statements of the faith of an individual. It is not being assumed that statements of belief made in a group are better than those held by an individual. Both are valid, and each depends upon the other.

Nevertheless, these two modes of belief tend to deal with different realms. Personal faith tends to focus on individual existence, and statements of belief held by groups are likely to focus on the existence of the group. In my strictly personal life, I struggle with problems of integrity, relationships with other selves and God, personal success or failure. As a citizen, I am part of a group which must reach decisions on such large-scale issues as the source, nature, and use of power in society, and the structure and use of the physical world. Many Protestants worship in churches which grew up outside the "establishment." These churches came into existence in order to protest the state churches of the establishment, or in a society so new and so unsettled that there was as yet no establishment. "Protest" churches tend to stress personal affairs which state churches sometimes ignore; but the protest churches also often tend to ignore the relationships of Christianity to society as a whole with which the state churches were preoccupied. Frontier churches were born when social structures were primitive and the needs of an individual dominated life. Thus, whether we Protestants worship in a protest church or a onetime frontier church, many of us have difficulty in believing that it is the business of Christianity to deal with the massive problems facing society as a whole today.

But ponder the meaning of the coronation ceremony. In the inauguration of a president of the United States, we install the victor in an election—a personal contest with another candidate. The ceremony is chiefly an individual triumph in which the newly elected president describes policies he hopes to follow. The ceremony itself has only a faint religious tinge. The ancient Israelite coronation ceremony was wholly different. It declared, in ancient and awful words, that the right of the king to rule came from God, and that the people whom he ruled were God's people. The king lived under a constant and an absolute restraint. He ruled God's people on God's behalf, not his own people on his own behalf. What would this mean if it were translated into modern political institutions? Politics would become a form of the Christian ministry in which misconduct would be an offense against God. Corruption would not be excused as long as it went undetected or was the conduct of a popular leader; it would always be a total evil, a misuse of the world God had created. And consider what it would mean in terms of the responsibility of the people of God to watch over, to support, or to condemn each elected official. Many of us think that such a change of mind on the part of Christians toward politics is long overdue.

Or ponder the meaning of the enthronement festival. The basic belief that lies behind it is that the whole earth is God's. If the Christian church in our day celebrated each year the enthronement of God as ruler of the universe, and attempted to understand what this rite meant in terms of Christian conduct, would there be any results in the lives of scientists, farmers, businessmen, housewives, governmental agencies dealing with natural resources, and all others who handle a fragment of a universe belonging to the divine King?

Understanding the psalms as cult liturgies opens up to us large areas in which we are called to serve God, by confronting us with ancient festivals in which God was related intimately to the daily lives of his people in ways we have forgotten, to our loss.

NOTES

1. See *The Book of Worship* (Nashville: The Methodist Publishing House, 1964, 1965), pp. 32-43.
2. Prefatory material on the book of Psalms is provided in the commentaries, which should also be consulted for information on individual psalms. The older commentaries use only literary and historical criticism. Among these, the best of the more detailed is C. A. Briggs, *A Critical and Exegetical Commentary on the Book of Psalms* (2 vols., New York: Charles Scribner's Sons, 1906-1907). See also W. E. Barnes, *The Psalms, with Introduction and Notes* (2 vols., New York: E. P. Dutton & Co., 1931); and Moses Buttenwieser, *The Psalms, Chronologically Treated with a New Translation* (Chicago: University of Chicago Press, 1938). For commentaries also using form criticism, see: W. O. E. Oesterley, *A Fresh Approach to the Psalms* (New York: Charles Scribner's Sons, 1937); A. Weiser, *The Psalms, a Commentary*, H. Hartwell, tr. (Philadelphia: The Westminster Press, 1962). Using form criticism but less detailed and intended for a less scholarly audience: E. A. Leslie, *The Psalms, Translated and Interpreted*. Some of the general books on the Psalms are quite useful, such as Samuel Terrien, *The Psalms and Their Meaning for Today* (Indianapolis: The Bobbs-Merrill Co., 1952); John Paterson, *The Praises of Israel: Studies Literary and Religious in the Psalms* (New York: Charles Scribner's Sons, 1950). Form criticism is so important in the study of the Psalms that a review of one or more of the following discussions of it might prove useful: A. Weiser, *The Old Testament: Its Formation and Development*, pp. 32-39; A. Bentzen, *Introduction to the Old Testament*, I, 146-67; Eissfeldt, *The Old Testament, an Introduction*, pp. 102-24.
3. Weiser, *The Psalms, a Commentary*, pp. 23-52, defends this view. Hans-Joachim Kraus, *Worship in Israel: A Cultic History of the Old Testament*, Geoffrey Buswell, tr. (Richmond: John Knox Press, 1966), defends the view taken here that there were several festivals. See especially pp. 134-236.
4. This ceremony has been reconstructed by G. von Rad from Old Testament references and Egyptian parallels in his "The Royal Ritual in Judah," in *The Problem of the Hexateuch and Other Essays*, pp. 222-31.
5. K. R. Crim, *The Royal Psalms*, presents a statement of the cultic significance of the king, pp. 15-68, and expounds ten psalms: 2, 18, 20,

21, 45, 72, 89, 101, 110, 144, and 2 Samuel 23:1-7 in the light of the view of the king he has given.

6. H. L. Ginsberg, "Ugaritic Myths, Epics, and Legends," in Pritchard, ed., *Ancient Near Eastern Texts*, p. 139; and *The Ancient Near East, an Anthology*, p. 110.
7. Ginsberg, in Pritchard, ed., *Ancient Near Eastern Texts*, p. 140, and in *The Ancient Near East, an Anthology*, p. 113. See note 5, chapter 1 for markings in the translation.
8. Sigmund Mowinckel, *The Psalms in Israel's Worship*, D. R. Ap-Thomas, tr. (2 vols., Nashville: Abingdon Press, 1962), I, 169-82.
9. *Ibid.*, I, 193 ff.; II, 4, 18-25.
10. O. Eissfeldt, *The Old Testament, an Introduction*, p. 115, note 44, enumerates forty psalms which one or another form critic has held to be an individual lament.

VII

ISRAEL'S SAGES

Three books in the Old Testament were the work of the sages, or the wise men. They are Job, Proverbs, and Ecclesiastes. The sages also wrote some of the psalms, such as psalm 1, and added passages to several of the prophetic books—such as Jeremiah 10:23-25; Hosea 14:9. Other collections of their work are the Wisdom of Sirach and the Wisdom of Solomon. Both of these are in the Apocrypha. The books of the Apocrypha are included in the Roman Catholic Old Testament but not in the Jewish Bible or the Protestant Old Testament.[1] In this chapter we will use only the three books first named, Job, Proverbs, and Ecclesiastes.

It is hard to be sure about the dates of these books. The sages did not discuss historical events in their writings, and we cannot use allusions to events for dating. The same rule applies here that holds good elsewhere in the Old Testament: these books are the work of many authors, as Proverbs 10:1; 24:23; 25:1 and 31:1 make clear. It is likely, therefore, that different parts of the books come from different times. One book, Ecclesiastes, uses words borrowed from Greek, and a strong Greek influence in Palestine came late in Old Testament history.

Many people find it easier to understand the wise men than the prophets, historians, or lawgivers of the Old Testament. In order to see why this is true, we need to describe the sages. Attempting to do this is like trying to put together a jigsaw puzzle with nine out of every ten pieces missing. The sages knew who they were, the people knew who they were, and no one took the trouble to explain the obvious.

Some things are fairly clear. Many of the proverbs in the book of Proverbs deal with the king or with the royal court (see for examples, Prov. 14:35; 16:10, 13, 15; 20:8; 22:29). Some of these report conduct proper for the king. Others describe how to behave in the presence of the king or how to be useful to a king. Proverbs 22:29 is an example of the last.

> Do you see a man skilful in his work?
> he will stand before kings;
> he will not stand before obscure men.

Furthermore, when we have descriptions of the wise men—as in the books of Job and Ecclesiastes—we are told that they were highly respected, sometimes wealthy, and were noted for their knowledge and wisdom. Job 29 is the fullest description of the standing of a wise man in his community given us in the Old Testament. The picture found in Ecclesiastes 1:12; 2:4-9; 12:9-10, tells us that this sage was a wealthy, well-educated ruler who both taught and wrote.

The scribes, a learned professional group, are mentioned fairly often in the Old Testament. David had an officer in his court called "the writer" or "the secretary" (2 Sam. 8:17; 20:25), and Solomon had two (1 Kings 4:3). During Isaiah's lifetime, King Hezekiah had a secretary, or scribe, named Shebna who managed the affairs of the king (Is. 22:15, 19-22; 36:3; 2 Kings 19:2). King Josiah sent his scribe, Shaphan, to get an accounting of the Temple finances. When Shaphan arrived, he was given a newly discovered book which he read and which he took to read to the king (2 Kings 22:3-10). He also was a member of the group sent to the prophetess Hulda (2 Kings 22:12-20), apparently as the personal representative of the king. Another scribe was Baruch, the secretary of the prophet Jeremiah. We are told how Jeremiah dictated his message to Baruch who copied it "with ink," and how Baruch then read it in public and to the princes (Jer. 36:4-8, 13-18).

A late description of David's administrative staff identifies one of the king's uncles, Jonathan, as "a counselor, being a man of understanding and a scribe" (1 Chron. 27:32). An even later reference to those who served the king as educated civil servants specifies that they were to be "youths without blemish, handsome and skillful in all wisdom, endowed with knowledge, understanding learning, and competent to serve in the king's palace." They were to be taught for three years, learning to speak, read, and write their master's language (Dan. 1:3-5).

This is not as complete information as we would like, but it is typical of all that we have. Fortunately, it all points in the same direction. The "wise" seem to have been those in ancient Israel who had an education which included a knowledge of reading, writing, and arithmetic. Some were educated for a profession. Some were wealthy enough to be able to afford a formal education for its own sake. Solomon was a representative of the latter group. Those who made a living with their education served others who lacked their formal training. By the nature of things, jobs like this would be found most often where records were kept, in the royal court or in a shrine. Thus the professional scribe would often be a part of the court.

A person cannot learn to read without having something to read, to speak without exercises in speaking, to write without lessons in composition. Some of the pupils being taught to read and write would end up in positions where they would need to know how to behave in fashionable society, how to keep secrets, how to manage affairs wisely. Would it be odd if the reading and writing lessons were also used to teach these other lessons? Thus it is reasonable to suspect that a series of proverbs, which describe proper conduct for a secretary serving a king, might have been in an exercise book for training royal secretaries.

Exercise books are only the start of an education. Once the start has been made, more can follow. We learned to read and write in the elementary grades. Unless we are teachers of children, we often take these skills so much for granted that it is hard to believe reading was ever difficult work for a fourth grader. As our mastery of the skills of communication increases, we can think more complex thoughts. This is one of the reasons education can be exciting. The struggle to understand becomes more satisfying as the material we are seeking to understand becomes more interesting.

The same thing seems to have happened in the wisdom movement. Teachers seem to have taken over the popular proverb as a tool to teach reading and writing. But this tool also helped them to teach ideas. Interest in ideas led them toward more and more complex ideas until finally we have the book of Job, one of the most fascinating, complex, and beautiful books in the history of literature. And the same interest in the world, which makes it possible for a person to write a good proverb, makes it possible for him to collect information. Solomon is described as having known three thousand proverbs, over a thousand songs, plus information about trees, animals, reptiles, and fish (1 Kings 4:32-33).[2]

If the picture of the wise man given here is correct, he often was a professional man, and the wisdom he learned provided the tools of his profession and the ideals he would need for his work. These ideals were personal. They were not intended to govern the life of the nation. A nation does not become a king's private secretary. From the beginning the wisdom movement was concerned with the life of the individual, not the cult in which the nation worshiped. This is the first reason we understand the wisdom books today so easily. We think of ourselves first as individuals. Only later do we think of ourselves as part of a group. We believe that only the individual thinks and is moral. A group has no conscience, makes no decisions, does not think. The authors of most of the Old Testament would disagree with these statements. They were aware of themselves chiefly as part of a group, and they thought and spoke as agents of that group. The writers of the wisdom books, however, were individualists, and we understand them.

The second reason we understand them is that they were interested in doing something that interests us also. Try to write a proverb of your own, which you think others would accept. When you get one which several people have said is good, recall the thinking you did in order to write it.

The kind of mind that produces and enjoys proverbs is the practical and the observing mind. This is the kind of intelligence needed by a farmer, mechanic, businessman, housewife, technician, or scientist—and by a good secretary, whether for a king or for a businessman. Here are several proverbs which reflect a good deal of shrewdness.

> The dread wrath of a king is like the growling of
>   a lion;
>   he who provokes him to anger forfeits his life.
> (Prov. 20:2.)

> Every way of a man is right in his own eyes,
>   but the Lord weighs the heart.
> (21:2.)

> A prudent man sees danger and hides himself;
>   but the simple go on, and suffer for it.
> (22:3.)

> It is better to live in a corner of the housetop
>   than in a house shared with a contentious
>   woman.
> (21:9; repeated in 25:24.)

Proverbs are attempts to say as much as possible in as few words as possible. They are intended to be read one at a time and pondered. Some of them are very apt, and part of the pleasure we take in them is discovering just how apt they are.

The third reason we understand the wisdom literature more easily than prophetic, historical, or legal writings in the Old Testament is that it is universal in origin and use. In the rest of the Old Testament, you have to learn something about the culture of the people who produced the literature in order really to understand what you are reading. Wisdom literature came into being in several different lands. That which we described as being the history of the wisdom movement in ancient Israel was only a part of a larger history going on also in Egypt and Babylonia. The

ideas, even collections of sayings, seem to have been passed from
one country to another. In Proverbs 22:20, for example, we are
told that we have a list of thirty sayings, but there aren't thirty.
The statement, however, does make sense when we learn that
Proverbs 22:17–24:11 is based upon a collection of thirty sayings
in an Egyptian collection called the "Instruction of Amen-em-opet."
Proverbs were international in origin. They fit men everywhere,
not just ancient Israelites.[3]

Finally, these books contain attempts to answer some questions
which sound as if they might have been asked today.

If we believe that there is a God, that he is good, that his will
for us is that we be good, and that he is powerful; what are we to
think when a good man suffers? If God rewards the good and
punishes the wicked, what are we to think when the righteous
seem to be punished and the wicked seem to be rewarded?

This question comes up repeatedly in the wisdom literature.
Here is an example.

> 11) And they [the wicked] say, "How can God know?
>   Is there knowledge in the Most High?"
> 12) Behold, these are the wicked;
>   always at ease, they increase in riches.
> 13) All in vain have I kept my heart clean
>   and washed my hands in innocence.
> 14) For all the day long I have been stricken,
>   and chastened every morning.
>   (Ps. 73:11-14.)

Psalm 37 also is a wisdom psalm. It gives one of the answers
people are still giving to this question.

> I have been young, and now am old;
>   yet I have not seen the righteous forsaken
>   or his children begging bread.
>   (Vs. 25.)

This is a denial that the righteous do suffer and that the wicked do prosper. It is not the only answer given, but the mere fact that it appears so often—four of the many examples are Proverbs 10:3; 11:8, 19; Job 34:5-12—is proof that the question was asked often. People do not rush about giving answers to questions that are not being asked.

This is precisely the kind of question we ask today. It is not easy to believe in the God who was the Father of our Lord Jesus Christ. Had all the millions who suffered and died in the two world wars of the first half of this century offended him? Had those killed in the bombings of Coventry, London, Berlin, Amsterdam, Leipzig, Hamburg, Tokyo, and Hiroshima angered God more than the people of San Francisco and Buffalo? Has everyone now living behind the Iron, or the Bamboo, Curtain sinned more than those who live in Sweden? What about the people crippled or killed in auto accidents, students growing up in areas where racial tension bars them from the education they need in a technological age? We have been told that only the sinful suffer. Were all the persons known by you to have died of cancer evil? We have been told that people of good character always find work. Does this include men who know nothing but the mining of coal which is now done more swiftly and cheaply by a machine? One such machine produces as much each hour as twelve hundred miners. Is the machine more righteous than the men, or its designers, or its owners? When an unemployed coal miner goes to Pittsburgh to find work and finds himself too old to be trained for a new job, is he experiencing the wrath of God? What about the executive displaced by a machine?

Many of us cannot escape the kinds of questions the sages tried to answer in the wisdom books. Whether we agree with their answers or not, the questions they asked make sense. We are asking the same questions ourselves.

These, then, are the reasons we find the wisdom books important: They deal with problems in the lives of individuals; In many ways, their authors thought as we think; Their conclusions had been worked out in many countries to fit the lives of men in many lands; And they asked the kind of basic questions we find ourselves asking.

All is not clear sailing, of course. We have been trained to read as swiftly as possible; the wisdom books should be read slowly. We live in the twentieth century of the Christian era; the authors of the wisdom books lived centuries before our era and used ancient Jewish figures of speech which we have some trouble understanding. How much sense would the phrase, "fish or cut bait," make to a man who had always lived in the desert? But we can overcome some of our difficulties. We can learn to read proverbs slowly and thoughtfully. We can suspend judgment on those passages we cannot understand until we have a chance to look them up. So now let us see what we can make of the wisdom books.

We will deal first with Proverbs, then with Job, and finally with Ecclesiastes. Each one of these books had several authors, and this will be important to remember when we turn to each book.

PROVERBS

We deal with Proverbs first because its message is the simplest, not because it is the oldest of the three.[4] If you decide to read the entire book, don't be surprised if some of the proverbs in it sound familiar. Some of these sayings are still being repeated. Several appear twice in this book, such as Proverbs 10:1 and 15:20; 19:5 and 19:9; and 21:9 and 25:24. In some cases, the same meaning is expressed in two proverbs in spite of minor changes in the wording, as in 16:2 and 21:2; 20:10 and 20:23; and 21:9 and 21:19. Sometimes similar phrases and figures of speech appear in two otherwise dissimilar proverbs, as in 25:5 and 29:14; 26:3 and 10:13; and 26:27 and 28:10. There are several collections of proverbs in the book, and a few of them appeared originally in more than one collection.

In general there are four kinds of material in the book.[5] The first and oldest is a series of shrewd, sometimes amusing, sayings which deal with daily problems. To find a group of these, read chapters 25 to 27. Here are a few examples.

> Like clouds and wind without rain
>> is a man who boasts of a gift he does
>>> not give.
>>>> (Prov. 25:14.)

> Like snow in summer or rain in harvest,
>> so honor is not fitting for a fool.
>>> (26:1.)

> Answer not a fool according to his folly,
>> lest you be like him yourself.
>>> (26:4.)

> Answer a fool according to his folly,
>> lest he be wise in his own eyes.
>>> (26:5.)

> The sluggard buries his hand in the dish;
>> it wears him out to bring it back to his
>>> mouth.
>>>> (26:15.)

> He who blesses his neighbor with a loud voice,
>> rising early in the morning,
>> will be counted as cursing.
>>> (27:14.)

Another group of proverbs is primarily religious. If you turn to Proverbs 10:1, you learn that you are starting to read a collection which once had the title, "The proverbs of Solomon." Here religious proverbs are mixed in with others in which religious themes—such as righteousness—play no part. You can see the contrast in verses 15 and 16 of chapter 10.

> 15) A rich man's wealth is his strong city;
>> the poverty of the poor is their ruin.

16) The wage of the righteous leads to life,
    the gain of the wicked to sin.

If you remember that each proverb is best studied alone, it follows that there is no connection between these two. They contradict each other unless you read one in the light of the other. But if you do read one in the light of the other, you find yourself faced with two proverbs which define the rich as righteous and the poor as wicked. Then these two proverbs conflict with Isaiah 53:9, where the wicked are equated with the rich. It is better to follow the rule and to read each proverb as it was intended to be read—by itself. Each proverb was produced separately. They then were collected, and the collections often contain proverbs which disagree —just as Proverbs 26:4 contradicts 26:5.

The religious proverbs in this part of the book generally argue that the righteous will prosper because of their righteousness, and that the wicked will suffer because of their wickedness. Here are a few examples.

> A wicked man earns deceptive wages,
>   but one who sows righteousness gets a
>   sure reward.
>
> (Prov. 11:18.)
>
> He who is steadfast in righteousness will live,
>   but he who pursues evil will die.
>
> (11:19.)
>
> Righteousness guards him whose way is upright,
>   but sin overthrows the wicked.
>
> (13:6.)

The difference between reading for pleasure and serious reading is that the serious reader is always looking for information and meaning. In a proverb the content is provided both by the author, as a result of his observations, and by the reader, who tests the proverbs in accordance with his observation of life. The question always is, Is this proverb true? This question is most important in the study of what has been called here the religious proverb, the proverb which claims that the righteous prosper and the wicked suffer. This is one of the most important questions anyone ever has to answer, and all of us must answer it whether we want to or not. Whether we talk about it or not, even whether we think about it or not, we answer through our conduct.

We have seen how the authors of some of the proverbs answered the question. Look now at Proverbs 30:1-9.

1) The words of Agur son of Jakeh of Maasa.

    The man says to Ithiel,
      to Ithiel and Ucal:
2) Surely I am too stupid to be a man.
    I have not the understanding of a man.
3) I have not learned wisdom,
    nor have I knowledge of the Holy One.
4) Who has ascended to heaven and come down?
    Who has gathered the wind in his fists?
Who has wrapped up the waters in a garment?
    Who has established all the ends of the
      earth?
What is his name, and what is his son's name?
    Surely you know!

5) Every word of God proves true;
    he is a shield to those who take refuge
      in him.
6) Do not add to his words,
    lest he rebuke you, and you be found
      a liar.
7) Two things I ask of thee;
    deny them not to me before I die:
8) Remove far from me falsehood and lying;
    give me neither poverty nor riches;
    feed me with the food that is needful
      for me,
9) lest I be full, and deny thee,

and say, "Who is the LORD?"
  or lest I be poor, and steal,
    and profane the name of my God.

This passage seems to contain the work of three authors, the second
and third of whom rejected the views of the first. Verses 1 to 4 were
the original; verses 5 and 6 were one corrective; verses 7 to 9 were
another corrective. Even in the ancient world, one way of dealing
with an independent thinker was to pretend that he had not
spoken. The debate reflected here—the struggle to identify and
to attest revelation—is the third type of material in the book of
Proverbs. There is relatively little of it here, but it becomes a major
theme in Job and Ecclesiastes.

The fourth part of the book of Proverbs is a series of hymns
and sermons praising wisdom. These lines are typical.

13) Happy is the man who finds wisdom,
        and the man who gets understanding,
14) for the gain from it is better than gain
          from silver
        and its profit better than gold.
15) She is more precious than jewels,
        and nothing you desire can compare with
          her.
16) Long life is in her right hand;
        in her left hand are riches and honor.
17) Her ways are ways of pleasantness,
        and all her paths are peace.
18) She is a tree of life to those who lay hold
          of her;
        those who hold her fast are called happy.
                          (Prov. 3:13-18.)

JOB

Let's turn now to the book of Job.[6] A few readings of this
book are usually enough to convince most people that several

cooks have contributed to this broth. The main part of the book—Job 3:1–42:6—is poetry. Job 1:1–2:13 and 42:7-17 are prose and tell a story complete in itself. The poetry also is complete in itself, and the prose contradicts the poetry. The theme of both seems to be the question, "Why do the righteous suffer?" The prose story answers, "We are being tested (Job 1:6–2:10), but all will turn out right in the end" (Job 42:10-17). Since the testing included the deaths of Job's wife and children, it is hard to stifle questions about the ethical sensitivity of those who would assert that the replacement of the dead family by another was making matters "turn out right in the end." It is certain that such moralism would have aroused the fury of the author of the poem. He gives an ambiguous answer to the question too complex to be stated briefly here. It isn't too odd that many scholars believe that the prose story and poem really do not belong together.[7]

There are also two parts of the poem which do not seem to belong to the rest. One is a long sermon by Elihu, a young and brash man (Job 32–37). Most of the poem reports an intense, bitter debate between Job—pictured as being a righteous man who has lost family, wealth, standing, and health—and three friends. This debate concludes, "The words of Job are ended" (Job 31:40). If you ignore Elihu's sermon, the poem continues without interruption in Job 38:1; "Then the LORD answered Job out of the whirlwind." This makes much better sense than to have Elihu, a complete stranger, repeat all the arguments which Job has already heard from his friends and has rejected. Many scholars, therefore, believe that chapters 32 to 37 were added later by someone who either did not understand the original poem or who disagreed sharply with it.

Chapter 28 also is questioned. Here the problem is not authorship. Many of those who feel that it does not belong to the poem of Job view it as having been written by the same author. The problem is simply that chapter 28, a hymn praising wisdom, does not fit where it now is.

Thus the main parts of the book which are thought not originally to have belonged to the poem of Job are 1:1–2:13; 28:1-28; 31:1–37:24; 42:7-17. The first and last of these, the prose story, is believed to have been an ancient folk story in which Job was the leading figure. The author of the poem may have used the legend as the point of departure for the creation of his epic poem, and a later editor merely inserted the poetic epic into the very old prose legend. The hymn praising wisdom (chap. 28) may have been composed by the author of the poem of Job, and inserted by an editor into the poem to preserve it. The sermon by Elihu is rather clearly an attempt, by someone holding views similar to those stated in the religious proverbs we have just examined, to correct the theological views of the author of the poem of Job.

The best way to study the poem of Job is to read it repeatedly. The outline is simple. Chapter 3 is the introduction. The conversation with the friends starts with chapter 4. Each friend tries to explain to Job why he is suffering. Job rejects each explanation. The debate becomes angry, and Job begins to accuse God.

The first friend, Eliphaz, begins:

> 2) If one ventures a word with you, will you
>   be offended?
>   Yet who can keep from speaking?
> 3) Behold, you have instructed many,
>   and you have strengthened the weak hands.
> 4) Your words have upheld him who was stumbling,
>   and you have made firm the feeble knees.
> 5) But now it has come to you, and you are
>   impatient;
>   it touches you, and you are dismayed.
> 6) Is not your fear of God your confidence,
>   and the integrity of your ways your hope?
>
> 7) Think now, who that was innocent ever
>   perished?
>   Or where were the upright cut off?

8) As I have seen, those who plow iniquity
   and sow trouble reap the same.
                                    (Job 4:2-8.)

If there is anything that is maddening, it is to receive in your hour
of need the same good advice you once gave others, and Job
replied testily:

14) He who withholds kindness from a friend
    foresakes the fear of the Almighty.
15) My brethren are treacherous as a torrent-bed,
    as freshets that pass away,

21) Such you have now become to me;
    you see my calamity, and are afraid.
22) Have I said, "Make me a gift"?
    Or, "From your wealth offer a bribe for me"?
23) Or, "Deliver me from the adversary's hand"?
    Or, "Ransom me from the hand of oppressors"?

24) Teach me, and I will be silent;
    make me understand how I have erred.
25) How forceful are honest words!
    But what does reproof from you reprove?
26) Do you think that you can reprove words,
    when the speech of a despairing man is wind?
27) You would even cast lots over the fatherless,
    and bargain over your friend.
28) But now, be pleased to look at me;
    for I will not lie to your face.
29) Turn, I pray, let no wrong be done.
    Turn now, my vindication is at stake.
30) Is there any wrong on my tongue?
    Cannot my taste discern calamity?
                                    (Job 6:14-15, 21-30.)

Unintimidated, each friend takes his turn. Bildad, sure that
God is just, suggests that the children for whom Job is responsible
may have sinned and urges Job to repent on their behalf.

3) Does God pervert justice?
    Or does the Almighty pervert the right?
4) If your children have sinned against him,
    he has delivered them into the power of their
        transgression.
5) If you will seek God
    and make supplication to the Almighty,
6) if you are pure and upright,
    surely then he will rouse himself for you
    and reward you with a rightful habitation.
                              (Job 8:3-6.)

Job is not greatly impressed. It is difficult to establish one's self as innocent when one's judge is he who accuses one of guilt.

15) Though I am innocent, I cannot answer him;
    I must appeal for mercy to my accuser.

19) If it is a contest of strength, behold him!
    If it is a matter of justice, who can
    summon him?
                            (Job 9:15, 19.)

Zophar, the third friend, attempts reason. He points out that the mere fact that Job is suffering proves that he also is sinful, since God is just. "Know then that God exacts of you less than your guilt deserves" (Job 11:6c). But the sinner can repent and know again divine favor (vss. 13-19). Job's reply might be called a bit caustic.

2) No doubt you are the people,
    and wisdom will die with you.
3) But I have understanding as well as you;
    I am not inferior to you.
    Who does not know such things as these?
4) I am a laughingstock to my friends;
    I, who called upon God and he answered me,
    a just and blameless man, am a laughingstock.

5) In the thought of one who is at ease there is
    contempt for misfortune;
    it is ready for those whose feet slip.
6) The tents of robbers are at peace,
    and those who provoke God are secure,
    those who are idolaters.[8]

(Job 12:2-6.)

Then Job cries:

But I would speak to the Almighty,
    and I desire to argue my case with God.
(Job 13:3.)

As the friends enter the second round of arguments, the discussion gets angrier, and Job repudiates his companions.

2) I have heard many such things;
    miserable comforters are you all.
3) Shall windy words have an end?
    Or what provokes you that you answer?
(Job 16:2-3.)

Finally, Job states his case against God.

4) As for me, is my complaint against man?
    Why should I not be impatient?
5) Look at me, and be appalled,
    and lay your hand upon your mouth.
6) When I think of it I am dismayed,
    and shuddering seizes my flesh.
7) Why do the wicked live,
    reach old age, and grow mighty in power?

17) How often is it that the lamp of the wicked is
    put out?
    That their calamity comes upon them?
    That God distributes pains in his anger?

22) Will any teach God knowledge,
    seeing that he judges those that are on
        high?
23) One dies in full prosperity,
    being wholly at ease and secure,
24) his body full of fat
    and the marrow of his bones moist.
25) Another dies in bitterness of soul,
    never having tasted of good.
26) They lie down alike in the dust,
    and the worms cover them.
                    (Job 21:4-7, 17, 22-26.)

Then he describes once more his innocence (Job 29:1–31:40) The poet then marks off the end of a major part of the epic with the sentence, "The words of Job are ended."

If we picture the poem of Job as a drama, there are two acts. We have just described the first, the argument between Job and his friends. The second act is a dialogue. It begins,

1) Then the Lord answered Job out of the whirlwind:
2) "Who is this that darkens counsel by words
    without knowledge?
3) Gird up your loins like a man,
    I will question you, and you shall declare
        to me."
                    (Job 38:1-3.)

A series of questions follow in which God asks Job if his knowledge of creation and his power over nature were greater than God's. This ends:

1) And the Lord said to Job:
2) "Shall a faultfinder contend with the
        Almighty?
    He who argues with God, let him answer it."

3) Then Job answered the Lᴏʀᴅ:
4) "Behold, I am of small account; what shall
    I answer thee?
    I lay my hand on my mouth.
5) I have spoken once, and I will not answer;
    twice, but I will proceed no further."
                                    (Job 40:1-5.)

A second time,

6) God answered Job out of the whirlwind:
7) "Gird up your loins like a man;
    I will question you, and you declare to me.
8) Will you even put me in the wrong?
    Will you condemn me that you may be justified?"
                                    (Job 40:6-8.)

Job now is asked whether he is wise enough to judge men and
powerful enough to restrain them, whether he can control the
chaos monster and thus sustain the world (Job 40:15-24 may be a
later addition). This series of questions ends with the closing
lines of the poem.

1) Then Job answered the Lᴏʀᴅ:
2) "I know that thou canst do all things,
    and that no purpose of thine can be
    thwarted.

3b) Therefore I have uttered what I did not
    understand,
    things too wonderful for me, which I
    did not know.

5) I had heard of thee by the hearing of
    the ear,
    but now my eye sees thee;
6) therefore I despise myself,
    and repent in dust and ashes.
                                    (Job 42:1-2, 3b, 5-6.)⁹

What does the poem of Job mean? It obviously is the most intense, most honest examination of the belief that the righteous prosper and the wicked suffer ever to be written. But what answer does it give to the question it raises? This is another of the problems raised in the study of the Old Testament for which there is no scholarly agreement. What follows, therefore, must be understood to be merely one answer out of many.

Scattered through Job's replies to his friends are several references to ancient Jewish legal procedures. Early in the discussion, Job points out that no one really could hope to be in the right in a dispute with God since God makes the rules, judges men by them, and carries out his judgments.

> 19) If it is a contest of strength, behold him!
>   If it is a matter of justice, who can
>   summon him?
>
> 32) For he is not a man, as I am, that I might
>   answer him,
>   that we should come to trial together.
> 33) There is no umpire between us,
>   who might lay his hand upon us both.
>   (Job 9:19, 32-33.)

Yet Job demands that God be brought to trial. First he demands a hearing before God.

> 20) Only grant two things to me,
>   then I will not hide myself from thy face:
> 21) withdraw thy hand far from me,
>   and let not dread of thee terrify me.
> 22) Then call, and I will answer;
>   or let me speak, and do thou reply to me.
> 23) How many are my iniquities and my sins?
>   Make me know my transgression and my sin.
>   (Job 13:20-23.)

Finally, Job makes a formal accusation against God.

Why are not times of judgment kept by the
  Almighty,
and why do those who know him never see
  his days?

(Job 24:1.)

Then he states the evidence upon which his accusation rests (Job 24:2-25). This recalls Absalom's accusation that David was not carrying out his duties as king (2 Sam. 15:1-6), and the legal situation is the same in both cases. Job then rests his own case against God with an extended, formal declaration of his own guiltlessness (Job 29:1–31:40).

The dramatic structure of the poem of Job is based on God's acceptance of the challenge. Job has presented his case before an unwilling, even horrified, jury of orthodox men who defend God throughout by denying frantically the plain facts of the case. By contrast, God shows himself so concerned with Job's demand for justice that "God answered Job out of the whirlwind."

At this point, we need to pause and examine another passage in the Old Testament which reports an accusation against God in the language of the law courts. Here, God, speaking through a prophet, himself is reporting the charge.

Thus says the LORD:
"What wrong did your fathers find in me
  that they went far from me,
and went after worthlessness, and became
  worthless?"

(Jer. 2:5.)

When legal procedures were used to describe the relationship between God and Israel, one change was needed. Two of the three parties in the trial were merged. When God was the accuser, he also was the judge who decided the case and carried out the sentence. When God was the accused, he was also the judge who decided the case and carried out the sentence. In

Jeremiah 2:5, we infer that Israel has accused God of faithlessness to the covenant. If God were faithless, if he failed to rule Israel as its divine King, Israel was no longer bound by its covenant with him and could seek a different God. The significance of the question which introduces the statement that Israel is faithless now becomes clear:

> What wrong did your fathers find in me
> that they went far from me?

It is being assumed that the people's repudiation of Yahweh was based upon its feeling that he had wronged it first.

But when the prophet pictured God as being tried for faithlessness, he also had to picture God as the judge before whom the trial was conducted. An odd situation results. As God starts his self-defense before himself as judge, he begins by reminding Israel of events in which he had acted as its divine King. At once, his self-defense becomes also an accusation of faithlessness against Israel (Jer. 2:5-12). [10]

In Job 38:1–41:34, God is pictured again as allowing himself to be put on trial. Here he replies to the accusation with a series of questions. Job is asked repeatedly whether he has the power and wisdom to act as God acts. When Job is forced to admit that he does not, he surrenders his claim against God. He has been forced to learn that his challenge to God's righteousness is actually a challenge to God's sovereignty. He who has the power to rule the world establishes the rules by which it is to be governed. Thus the basic question faced by the book is seen to be this: Who governs the universe, God or Job?

If this understanding of the poem is correct, it raises a question so basic that we rarely discuss it with anything more than slogans and clichés. How much is man actually the measure of all things? How much must man accept the conditions of his existence, and how much right has he to demand that those conditions be changed? For thousands of years, our forefathers had to accept the conditions of their existence and knew it. Today, we have become confused by our science and technology. Because we can do many things, we conclude that we can do all things. We seem unable to see that all that has changed in our time is that our knowledge of the conditions of our existence has changed. We are just as much bound by what we are learning to be true of the universe in which we have been placed as our fathers knew themselves to be bound by the universe as they understood it. The discovery of a "scientific law" does not free man from the rule of the divine Lawgiver who ordained that law. Man did not create the law; he discovered it. He has merely discovered another of the conditions of his existence.

It is hard to read the poem of Job without suspecting uneasily that its author would be as impatient with the superficiality of our answer to the basic question he raised as he was with the answers given by the devout and orthodox Jews of his own day. Basically, he seems to be telling us that we must question the answers we give, so rigorously and so honestly that we are driven to give them up, one after the other. In the end, if we are sufficiently honest in our struggle with our slogans and sufficiently realistic of our view of the world in which we live, we *may* find ourselves confronted by a theophany, the direct personal knowledge of a reality so vast that it lies beyond either theism or atheism. Then the ultimate question of our existence becomes: How do I live with this knowledge?

ECCLESIASTES

The last of the three wisdom books to be discussed here is Ecclesiastes.[11] Since some of the words in this book are Greek, and since Greek culture made itself felt in Palestine only late in Old Testament times, this book is believed to be one of the last in the Old Testament to have been written. It also deals with the problem found in the other two books we have studied, but in a slightly different way. The question remains, Does God reward the righteous and punish the wicked? But the way it is asked sounds almost as if it had been asked just yesterday: Can I discover out of my own experience and thought about that experience what righteousness is? The theme of the original book of Ecclesiastes was the value of trying to find righteousness through wisdom.

The author tried pleasure and wealth (Eccl. 2:1-11), work (Eccl. 2:18-23) and justice (Eccl. 4:1-3). In none of these could he find the will of God. All were "vanity." Finally, he was driven to the conclusion:

(18) I said in my heart with regard to the sons of men that God is testing them to show them that they are but beasts. (19) For the fate of the sons of men and the fate of beasts is the same; as one dies, so dies the other. They all have the same breath, and man has no advantage over the beasts; for all is vanity. (Eccl. 3:18-19.)

This writing outraged many ancient Jews, and they added to it so much that recovering the original writing has become difficult. This writer did not deny that God existed. He merely denied that man ever knew what the will of God was. If man could not know what God wanted done, there was no such thing as righteousness or sin. Man was merely another animal. "There is nothing better for a man than that he should eat and drink, and find enjoyment in his toil" (Eccl. 2:24a). This is the end of religion. Religion is not only belief in God; it is also the attempt to obey God's will. This writer answered the question, "Do the righteous prosper and the wicked suffer" by replying, "We do not know the will of God. Therefore there is neither righteous nor wicked."

SUMMARY

We have traced one question through three Old Testament wisdom books, and we are now able to summarize. It is now clear that the question, "Do the righteous prosper and the wicked suffer?" really has two parts: "Can we learn what is right in order to be counted righteous by God?" and, "Is doing what we believe to be right worthwhile?"

We found four definitions of righteousness and four definitions of divine reward in the wisdom literature. These four compete with one another for our acceptance today just as strongly as they did when these books were first written.

1) Righteousness is "doing what comes naturally." It is being a healthy animal. The reward is being a healthy animal.
2) Righteousness is common sense. The reward is keeping out of trouble.
3) Righteousness is obedience to rules believed to have come from God. Reward is long life, wealth, public respect.
4) Righteousness is self-honesty and integrity in viewing the world in which one is placed. The reward may be life changed by the awesome knowledge of the presence of God.

The first of these was defended by the original author of Ecclesiastes, the second by the authors of the oldest collection in the book of Proverbs, the third by the authors of the religious proverbs, as well as by the authors of the additions in the books of Job and Ecclesiastes, and the fourth is defended by the authors of the poem of Job and psalm 73.

All four have to be judged in the same way. It is not a question of which is the easiest to understand. It is a question of which is right. If you decide that it is true that there is nothing more to your existence than to be a healthy or a sick animal, then the first statement of righteousness and reward is correct. If you have discovered that all our answers fall far short of the complexity and magnitude of reality, you may be on the verge of discovering what life is like when lived—as the authors of the Old Testament would state it—before the face of the living God.

NOTES

1. The Apocrypha is available in all the major English, Protestant versions, either bound separately or included between the Old and New Testa-

ments. For two recent translations see *The Apocrypha, an American Translation,* Edgar J. Goodspeed, tr. (Chicago: University of Chicago Press, 1938), and *The Apocrypha, Revised Standard Version* (New York: Thomas Nelson & Sons, 1957).

2. See Sheldon H. Blank, "Wisdom," and Matthew Black, "Scribe," *The Interpreter's Dictionary of the Bible;* and H. Wheeler Robinson, *Inspiration and Revelation in the Old Testament,* pp. 231-40.

3. John A. Wilson, tr., "The Instruction of Amen-em-opet," in Pritchard, ed., *Ancient Near Eastern Texts,* pp. 421-24; and *The Ancient Near East, an Anthology,* pp. 237-43. For the discussions of the international scope of the wisdom movement, see J. Coert Rylaarsdam, *Revelation in Jewish Wisdom Literature* (Chicago: University of Chicago Press, 1946), pp. 1-17. Harry Ranston, *Ecclesiastes and the Early Greek Wisdom Literature* (London: The Epworth Press, 1925), is an example of the kind of detailed studies that are available.

4. There are no good, recent, detailed commentaries in English on the book of Proverbs. The best recent work is R. B. Y. Scott, *Proverbs, Ecclesiastes; Translated with an Introduction and Notes* ("The Anchor Bible" [Garden City: Doubleday & Company, 1965]), an excellent translation but not a detailed commentary. Older commentaries are more detailed. See W. O. E. Oesterley, *The Book of Proverbs, with Introduction and Notes* (New York: E. P. Dutton & Co., 1929); and C. H. Toy, *A Critical and Exegetical Commentary on Proverbs* (New York: Charles Scribner's Sons, 1899).

5. R. Pfeiffer, *Introduction to the Old Testament,* pp. 645 ff., gives eight subdivisions in the book which served as the basis for this classification of the contents, O. Eissefeldt, *The Old Testament, an Introduction,* pp. 472-77, proposes seven collections which again can be reduced to the four types of material suggested here.

6. The literature on the book of Job is so large that only a sampling can be given here. Marvin H. Pope, *Job, Translated with an Introduction and Notes* ("The Anchor Bible" [Garden City: Doubleday & Company, 1965]), contains a wealth of data from archaeological and linguistic studies. Samuel Terrien, "Job, Introduction and Exegesis," *The Interpreter's Bible,* III, 877-1198, is an existentialist and form critical analysis. Morris Jastrow, *The Book of Job: Its Origin, Growth and Interpretation* (Philadelphia: J. B. Lippincott, 1920), and C. J. Ball, *The Book of Job, a Revised Text and Version* (Oxford: The Clarendon Press, 1922), are examples of older, detailed commentaries based on the use of literary and historical criticism. Briefer, older commentaries include A. B. Davidson, *The Book of Job* ("The Cambridge Bible for Schools and Colleges" [Cambridge: Cambridge University Press, 1891]); and A. S. Peake, *Job: Introduction, Revised Version with Notes and Index* ("The New Century Bible" [New York: Henry Frowde, 1905]). Representative of books about Job which are not commentaries:

Samuel Terrien, *Job: Poet of Existence* (Indianapolis: Bobbs-Merrill Co., 1957); and E. G. H. Kraeling, *The Book of the Ways of God* (New York: Charles Scribner's Sons, 1939). The book also has been made into a play: Archibald McLeish, *J. B.: A Play in Verse* (Boston: Houghton Mifflin Company, 1958). I find the original more provocative.

7. All the commentaries just listed discuss this (Pope ambiguously), and discussions of it are also to be found in all introductions to the Old Testament. Thus see Pfeiffer, *Introduction to the Old Testament,* pp. 667-75, and Eissfeldt, *The Old Testament, an Introduction,* pp. 456-66.

8. The Revised Standard Version translates the last line of verse 6, "who bring their god in their hand." These would be persons who were idol worshipers, and I have translated the phrase simply as "idolaters."

9. Materials omitted here are judged to be either later intrusions or to be displaced. There is a good deal of confusion at this point in the Hebrew text of Job. See the commentaries for discussions of the problems.

10. This reconstruction is a result of proposals made by Eberhard von Waldow, *Der traditionsgeschichtliche Hintergrund der prophetischen Gerichtsreden* (Berlin: Alfred Töpelmann, 1963), esp. pp. 32-33. Neither this work, nor any other dealing with the use of legal forms in prophetic oracles of judgment, is available in English translation.

11. Commentaries on Ecclesiastes include Scott, *Proverbs, Ecclesiastes;* O. S. Rankin, "Ecclesiastes: Introduction and Exegesis," *The Interpreter's Bible,* V, 3-88; Robert Gordis, *Koheleth—the Man and His World* ([published for *The Jewish Theological Seminary of America*]; New York: Bloch Publishing Co., 1955); Morris Jastrow, *A Gentle Cynic, Being the Book of Koheleth, Commonly Known as Ecclesiastes, Stripped of Later Additions* (Philadelphia: J. B. Lippincott, 1919), an extreme use of literary criticism; and G. A. Burton, *A Critical and Exegetical Commentary on the Book of Ecclesiastes* (New York: Charles Scribner's Sons, 1908).

VIII

IS THE BIBLE TRUE?

There was a time when Christians believed that every statement in the Bible was true. Biblical writers spoke truthfully not only of God, but also of the creation of the universe, the history of mankind, and the mysteries of nature. Scripture had been dictated by the Holy Spirit. It was without error.

The Renaissance and the scientific revolution have changed this for many Christians. Our confidence in the truthfulness of Scripture now is clouded over by doubt. Once an apt quotation from the Bible proved true or false a statement from any other source. Today the reverse often is true. We welcome, more or less openly, scientific confirmation that a biblical statement is true, whether it be a report of historical fact confirmed by archaeology or an insight into human nature confirmed by psychology.

We have responded to the change in the status of Scripture in many ways, the range of which is to be seen in a description of the two extremes. On the one hand, there are many Christians who have turned to modern thought for their knowledge of truth and to modern art for their description of truth. For these, the Bible is useful only when it states more artistically than other media truths established by modern thought. Those who prefer Archibald MacLeish's *J. B.* to the book of Job might represent this faction for us, since Mr. MacLeish removed God from the center of the book of Job when he rewrote it to make it a description of the human situation.

The opposite wing of the Christian community has responded to the deterioration in the status of the Bible as the book of truth by a vigorous attempt to "prove" it true in external details. In its most popular form, this activity has been the use of archaeology to prove the Bible. Each of the extremes being described here includes many variations, and Joseph P. Free, of Wheaton College, represents only one of several positions among those seeking to prove the Bible true through archaeology. He once described the value of archaeology in these words:

> . . . archaeology illuminates the text of the Scriptures and so makes valuable contributions to the fields of Biblical interpretation and exegesis. In addition . . . archaeology has confirmed countless passages which have been rejected by critics as unhistorical or contradictory to known facts.[1]

There is a clarity in this position which is appealing. Professor Free continued:

> The Bible is an historical book, and the great truths of Christianity are founded upon the historic facts revealed therein. . . . The accuracy and historicity of the Scriptures as God's Word and as His unique revelation has been denied by the destructive critic. . . . Yet archaeological discoveries have shown that these critical charges and countless others are wrong and that the Bible is trustworthy in the very statements which have been set aside as untrustworthy.[2]

A more moderate and more typical view is given by Jack Finegan, writing about the problems surrounding the historicity of the person and deeds of Moses.

> While there are certainly evidences of compilation in the Pentateuch, and while the materials therein must surely have been handed down over a perod of time, the most important consideration . . . would seem to be . . . whether the transmitted materials actually fit the time they purport to tell about.[3]

The answer given here by Professor Finegan—as in his other books—is affirmative.

It seems to me that those who have embraced modern quests for truth, and have preserved the Bible only as a literary work, have given up so much that it may be questioned whether they are

Christian any longer. One can agree fully with their respect for modern thought, as well as with their belief that our knowledge of truth will not be inconsistent within itself. Nevertheless, the Hebrew-Christian tradition in its normative form has conflicted with the demands of every culture in which its believers have lived. The basic assertion underlying all the Bible—and underlying the traditional place of Scripture in Judaism and Christianity—is that there is here a knowledge of the ways of God with men which overrides all cultures and all knowledge achieved by man alone. We face a constant struggle to identify the culture-transcending elements in Scripture, but abandoning the struggle is a surrender to culture.

This is a struggle which goes back at least as far as the Old Testament prophets, if not farther. The cultures men construct have always gained part of their effectiveness by rejecting alien viewpoints from which cultural criticism might arise. This has also been the source of much of the self-destructiveness found in culture. Since a knowledge of God transcending all culture is the most alien viewpoint possible, the most constant element in the history of each culture which has confronted Judaism and Christianity has been the attempt of each such culture to deny, or to domesticate, the transcendent claims of the Hebrew-Christian tradition. We need only to ponder the mounting stridency of the cultural assault on Christianity in our day to understand the antagonisms our spiritual forefathers confronted.

The issue is not whether rigorous thought about the Bible, compatible with the modern mood, will be permitted. Many biblical scholars and theologians are far more rigorous, critical, and sophisticated than the spokesmen for modernized, traditionless "religion." The issue is the degree to which it is possible for man to be confronted by a knowledge of God which transcends even the best of modern thought, a knowledge which confronts man so starkly and with such authority that it makes absolute demands upon him. The issue cannot be settled by dismissing the Bible, its most powerful expression, as an interesting but curious antiquity. This is merely retreat from the question.

Yet it also seems to me that those who have turned to archaeological research to prove the details of the biblical record—and thereby to prove the whole of that record—are equally wrong. There are three serious problems here.

The first is the error of thinking that proving some of the details in an account to be true proves the account as a whole to be true. All of us have been guilty of this many times. Historians have long argued that incorrectness in minor details undermines reliability, regardless of the accuracy of the report of other details. The careful historian concludes from such a mixture of error and truth that the narrative being studied is unreliable. It is the mixture of error and truth that makes the account untrustworthy, and merely establishing that there is some truth present does not eliminate the errors present.

When, therefore, archaeologists recover ancient Hittite laws of land ownership, which explain why trees were listed in the description of land purchased for a tomb (Gen. 23:17),[4] they have not proved the historicity of Abraham by proving the reliability of this detail.[5] Doubt of the historicity of the Abrahamic narratives has never depended upon questioning this detail. Thus establishing as possible the legal practice reported in the purchase of land in one of the Abrahamic narratives is a "proof" which is irrelevant to the questions being asked. All that has been proved is that memories of Hittite laws governing sales of land survived in Genesis 23:17.

The second error is failing to remember that archaeological proof gives probability only—just as does any other form of historical proof—and that the will to believe or to disbelieve adds to, or subtracts from, the probability. Enthusiasm for one's field, or the zeal of piety, has laid a heavy thumb in the scales when many statements about archaeological proof of the Bible have been written.

The identity of the builder of the Siloam Tunnel illustrates this. A somewhat damaged inscription was found in 1880 in the wall of a tunnel leading from the Gihon Spring through Ophel— the hill on which ancient Jerusalem was built—to the Pool of Siloam inside the old city's walls. All subsequent studies of the area are agreed that the tunnel was cut to lead water, from the spring outside the ancient city's walls, inside the city so that its defenders would have water during siege. Who ordered the tunnel cut?

We are told in 2 Kings 20:20 that King Hezekiah "made the pool and the conduit and brought water into the city." The inscription in translation reads:

[. . . when] (the tunnel) was driven through. And this was the way in which it was cut through:—While [. . .] (were) still [. . .] axe(s), each man toward his fellow, and while there were still three cubits to be cut through, [there was heard] the voice of a man calling to his fellow, for there was *an overlap* in the rock on the right [and on the left]. And when the tunnel was driven through, the quarrymen hewed (the rock), each man toward his fellow, axe against axe; and the water flowed from the spring toward the reservoir for 1,200 cubits, and the height of the rock above the head(s) of the quarrymen was 100 cubits.[6]

Thus, the inscription from inside the tunnel does not now give the name of the king who ordered the work done. It should also be noted that Isaiah was ordered to meet Ahaz, Hezekiah's father, "at the end of the conduit of the upper pool on the highway to the Fuller's Field" (Is. 7:3).

Many reporting on the tunnel and its inscription identify Hezekiah as the builder without comment or qualification,[7] but one scholar wrote, "The script and the idiom . . . indicate the period of Hezekiah, to whom such works are attributed." [8] The claim that Palestinian archaeology is proving the Bible would be made far less often if its discoveries were reported with this precision.

The third problem raised by the current attempt to prove the

Bible is suggested by G. Ernest Wright. After insisting on the need to study the historicity of the Scriptures of a faith based on historical revelation, and after affirming his confidence that archaeology can assist, he writes:

. . . . in addition there is in the Bible an interpretation of events and experience which is not subject to historical or archaeological testing. . . .
Hence the biblical archaeologist is definitely limited in the work which
he can do. He cannot prove that the Bible is "true," but he can and has
illuminated the historical setting.[9]

At the very least, the "truth" of the Bible involves the question of whether or not Amos was right when he proclaimed as God's word.

> But let justice roll down like waters,
>   and righteousness like an ever-flowing stream.
>   (Amos 5:24.)

Any alleged proof of the Bible which does not confront us with this dimension is blasphemy and self-deception.

Much that is useful, as well as some that is unreliable, has come out of the attempt to restore the Bible to its former preeminence. In my judgment, the attempt at its best has dealt with problems on the fringe of the issue. At its worst, it has been another means by which Christians have evaded the absolute demands of God mediated through Scripture.

Both those who have replaced the Bible with modern knowledge, and those who have tried to restore our confidence in its statements about externalities, have failed to take into account the nature of historical knowledge. This is not too surprising in a century which is more conscious of the recent discoveries of science than of the wisdom of the past, and in a nation which has only a short history but—God willing—a long future. But the Bible does portray a historical revelation. It has to be understood on its own terms, or it is not understood. Those terms are given in a description of the nature of historical knowledge.

It was said in an earlier chapter that man is a historical creature. An examination of this statement helps clarify the nature of historical knowledge.

We begin by asking what it is that sets man apart from other living beings. It is clear that we are warm-blooded mammals, but we share this distinction with nonhumans. This is not what makes us uniquely human. We live as biological organisms in a strange way. Like many other mobile land-life forms, we need shelter. Unlike the snake in its hole, the gopher in its burrow, or the bear in a cave, we build shelters of infinite variety out of materials which we have processed, improved, or invented. We eat food, as do all other life forms, but some of it we have improved, some we have created, and most of it we have prepared. Beef Stroganov is not found *au naturel!* This points toward a unique trait of our existence: We live in a culture which we have created.

We are culture-creating mammals, but this is not a full description of our uniqueness. It is true that we live in cultures we have made, but it also is true that we are constantly making choices within cultures.

As commonplace an example as a man turning off an alarm clock to go back to sleep demonstrates our use of the ability to make choices. The Russian psychologist Pavlov discovered that he could train dogs to drool by striking a tuning fork each time the dogs were fed meat powder. After this had gone on long enough to train the dogs, they drooled whenever the tuning fork was struck, whether or not meat powder was given them. Both Pavlov's dogs and the sleeping man responded to a ringing sound, but the nature of their responses differed. The dogs reacted. Once trained, they always drooled. The man awakened, understood the situation, saw choices present, and decided to return to sleep. A substantial amount of true freedom of choice is part of human existence.

Thus our creation of culture and our exercise of freedom of

choice within it are uniquely human. One of these, the creating of culture, points toward a third of man's traits.

The origins of culture building seem to be three: making and using tools, gregariousness, and memory. The first of these has been blamed on thumbs so jointed that we can grasp more efficiently than other mammals. The second has been attributed by at least one satirist to our simian ancestry. It is the third that is the most astounding and most important.

Animals can be trained to perform tricks which are amazing— for animals—but the average ten-year-old child has memorized a complex of cultural data so vast that it sets him off permanently and decisively from all other mammals. The list of learned cultural elements used daily is so great that it cannot be tabulated. We would have to include language, signs, customs, rules of conduct, ways of playing, working, eating, sleeping, our social structures, modes of dress, tools, traditions of craftsmanship, the core content of all branches of learning, the skills and conventions of all modes of artistic expression, and even taste in food. We move about easily and naturally in a universe of norms and possibilities which we have memorized so well that they seem natural to us. It is true that we have to use our biological inheritance as the base upon which culture is built. It also is true that groups construct culture. But unless one generation could teach the following generation, no culture would be possible. Complex civilizations— even primitive ones—do not arise in one generation.

An example of this will be helpful. When we want to communicate, we use speech and gesture. At once we face a choice: we can use correct English, slang, or a private vocabulary made up on the spot. If we use correct English or slang, we are depending on memory, even though one of the distinctions between them is that correct English has a longer history. Some slang is very old, but the grammatical forms and many of the roots of the words used in proper speech go back to ancient Latin and Greek.[10] Both correct English and slang are learned, by the speaker and listener. But if I attempt to communicate by a private language which I have invented on the spot, I make myself understood only because I also use nonverbal means of communication such as tone of voice, gesture, facial expression. Otherwise my private language would communicate nothing.

Recollection in the form of reliving a well-learned past thus seems to be basic in all uniquely human existence. It is reliving because it is an act, carried out in the present to meet the conditions of the present, which uses a wealth of material inherited from the past.

An example closer to our use of the Bible is now possible. If I reenact Independence Day, the following elements are present. I am so well informed of the events surrounding the signing and proclamation of the Declaration of Independence that I know them intellectually. My intellectual knowledge is so much a part of me, however, that I identify with the original happenings both in thought and feeling. Thus I move from mere knowledge about the past toward participation in it. My participation then becomes reenactment when I find myself so gripped by the mighty deeds out of which the independence of my nation emerged that I find myself seeing problems facing my generation as opportunities to relive this hallowed past. Now I hear, "We hold these truths to be self-evident, that all men are created equal," not only in terms of the struggle between colonial and British governments, but also in the struggle between Negro and Caucasian, and in the inequities that separate slum child from suburbanite child.

This is not historical determinism. There is no cosmic law which demands that I reenact one particular past. I can decide to learn a new language, emigrate and become a citizen of an adopted country, and change my religion. We are constantly deciding between various "pasts," and this use of our freedom is one of the ways that we create in the present the past toward which unborn generations will look.

Thus recollection is living each "today" in such a way that it becomes the fulfillment of the past. This is historical existence, the uniquely human form of existence.

In this understanding of ourselves, we need to bear constantly in mind the difference between fantasy and the past. All of us should have inherited from childhood the golden world of fantasy— of chivalrous knights on great horses, lovely princesses in distress, wise kings, evil queens, castles, elves and gnomes—and few of us want to give up this part of ourselves. But the past, out of which we live in the present, is the world of fact. Had the world of fantasy ever existed, men would have been so satisfied by it that the modern world would never have come to birth. Our present looks back to the peasants' revolt, the wars of religion, the rise of nation states and national languages, the collapse of the medieval synthesis, and the rise of the new learning.[11] It would be safe— I believe—to define personal and group health partly in terms of the degree to which the present is the reliving of a real past. We cannot free ourselves from the difficult, often troublesome, search for the facts of our past, least of all in our study of the Bible.

Furthermore, we need knowledge of our complete past, not merely those fragments of it which are compatible with the latest fad. This means that we are concerned both with happenings and with the meanings attached to them. There is adequate reason to believe that some Israelites who were impressed into slavery in Egypt escaped and came finally into Palestine and freedom. This sequence might be called a happening. But the happening becomes an event when meaning is seen in it. That meaning is stated repeatedly in the Old Testament and most tersely in the title given God, "I am the Lord, who brought you up out of Egypt." The happening became event when it was understood to be divine intervention. This is the past we reenact, and we are not actually dealing with the past unless we are trying to cope with its events in all their fullness. Consider some of the breadth and depth of this one "event" as it reappears constantly throughout the Old Testament: the exodus and the entry into Palestine under divine guidance become the basis for belief in a royal covenant between Yahweh and Israel. The royal covenant contains within itself the structures for making vivid the conviction that Yahweh had the right to make demands upon his people. Obedience to those royal demands was believed to bring blessing, but disobedience was felt to bring woe. The history of Israel is about all this, not merely the concrete details of individual happenings which might be reflected in the strata of a buried city. History is an incredible tapestry of men responding to happenings with understanding, forming events, and then creating new happenings by acting upon the previous events. It is into all this that we enter as we accept our historical inheritance.

When we ask whether an account of the past be true, we are asking how we fulfill our capacity for historical existence. On the practical level, the answer is to use all the methods of teaching the whole self—the mind, the will, and the emotions—by ways increasingly well-known today. We need to study a serious and responsible account of our past. We should use private study, group discussion, formal classes, dramatic reconstructions, visual aids. Even the study and work needed to reconstruct the common household articles of biblical antiquity—lamps, cooking pots, spinning whorls, and slings—helps. All forms of learning which involve us, the learners, are particularly useful. At some point, however, we need to mature and to pass to that kind of study of the past which becomes the attempt to act consciously upon it in the present. As we come to understand more and more clearly what the prophets were telling their generation about the viciousness of making gods of human desires, we should begin to detect and oppose the desires of our own generation to worship idols it has created. As we come to understand more and more clearly precisely what the laws of ancient Israel were intended to do, we should be pondering ways and means of achieving similar goals in the laws of our society. Thus the mechanism for historical existence is the use of all methods known to us for achieving the total involvement of the student in the study. It might be helpful to describe the difference between older and newer views of education in this way: we thought once that a student learned by learning about something outside himself; we know now that a student learns by entering into that which he seeks to learn. We learn the past by entering into it.

It is at this point that we finally are ready to be confronted by the question of the truth of the Bible. There is a large amount of scientific knowledge about childbirth. Much of it is correct, some of it is enigmatic, much of it is valuable. But there is a level of truth about childbearing which even the most brilliant woman physician will learn only by bearing children. The truth of the Bible belongs to this order of truth. Biblical scholarship produces truths about the Bible—along with much error, undoubtedly—but in the end all this scholarship has been undertaken in order to help us become engaged in a historical existence with the Bible in order to be confronted by the truth of the Bible. At that point it must commend itself, or no argument can ever commend it. But when it does commend itself to us, we have entered into new life. We will once again have heard the ancient promise, "I will be your God," and we will have answered, "And we will be your people."

NOTES

1. Joseph P. Free, *Archaeology and Bible History* (Wheaton, Ill.: Van Kampen Press, 1950), p. 1.
2. *Ibid.*, pp. 1-2.
3. Jack Finegan, *Let My People Go, a Journey Through Exodus* (New York: Harper & Row, 1963), p. 40.
4. Finegan, *Light from Ancient Past*, p. 146.
5. Werner Keller, *The Bible as History*, William Neil, tr. (New York: William Morrow & Co., 1956), wrote: "Here [Mamre] he gained possession of the first piece of land from the Hittites (Gen. 23) in order to provide a rock tomb for his wife Sarah. . . . He too was buried in the same sepulcher. (Gen. 25:9-10.) Excavations appear to confirm these Biblical statements, too, about the father of the patriarchs." (P. 83.)
6. William F. Albright, "Palestinian Inscriptions," in Pritchard, ed., *Ancient Near Eastern Texts*, p. 321; and *The Ancient Near East, an Anthology*, p. 212. See note 5, chapter 1 for markings in the translation.

The limestone in which the tunnel was carved is soft when first exposed to air, and carving it out with axes is entirely possible.

7. E.g., in Finegan, *Light from the Ancient Past,* p. 191.
8. Gray, *Archaeology in the Old Testament World,* pp. 155-56.
9. Wright, *Biblical Archaeology,* p. 18.
10. This is true even in the meanings of words, as a book like Mario Pei, *The Story of English* (Philadelphia: J. B. Lippincott Co., 1952), proves. This title is now available in paperback.
11. Contrast the world reported with delightful whimsy by T. H. White, *The Sword and the Stone* (New York: G. P. Putnam's Sons, 1939), with the world reported by the scholarship of G. G. Coulton, *Medieval Panorama: The English Scene from Conquest to Reformation* (New York: The Macmillan Company, 1938).

INDEX OF BIBLICAL QUOTATIONS

GENERAL INDEX

221